Praise for *Achieving Chastity in an Unchaste World*

"This little book gives excellent suggestions for effectively overcoming sexual temptations and especially addictions. Although written from a spiritual point of view, it is consistent with the best thinking in contemporary cognitive therapy approaches. It effectively brings spirituality and morality together with the best contemporary psychological thinking."

—***Fr. Benedict J. Groeschel, C.F.R.,***
Founding friar, Franciscan Friars of the Renewal

"Fr. Thomas Morrow, author of *Christian Courtship in an Oversexed World*, has come through with another very helpful book. After describing the problem in his introduction, Fr. Morrow makes superb use of the thought of John Paul II in his pre-papal book *Love and Responsibility* and in his marvelous Wednesday audiences on the theology of the body to help his readers come to see the tremendous value of the virtue of chastity, which enables us to come into possession of our sexual desires and not be possessed by them so that we can give ourselves away to others in love.

This eminently practical book, rooted in Fr. Morrow's pastoral experience, especially with homosexually oriented persons seeking to be chaste, is filled with useful advice. To overcome sexual addictions, one needs God's grace, prayer, good counseling, and a good support group.

Fr. Morrow's book should give persons who are sexually addicted great hope and those who love and advise them wonderful insights. I warmly recommend it."

— ***William E. May,*** Professor Emeritus, Pontifical John Paul II Institute for Studies on Marriage and Family, The Catholic University of America

"Fr. Tom Morrow's book is a real contribution to the pastoral care of persons with sexual addictions. While psychologists and psychiatrists will trace the dynamics of addiction to its origins to help the person know how he came to this condition, Fr. Morrow concentrates on presenting a spiritual strategy that will help the person on the long road back to inner freedom. That strategy includes not only deep honesty with oneself but also a life of reflective prayer, known as 'prayer of the heart.' From his pastoral experience over the years, Fr. Morrow has developed spiritual insights into the soul of the addict, which other spiritual directors will find spiritually profitable."

—***Fr. John F. Harvey, O.S.F.S.,***
Founder, Courage International

Achieving Chastity in an Unchaste World

Rev. T.G. Morrow

Achieving Chastity in an Unchaste World

SOPHIA INSTITUTE PRESS
Manchester, New Hampshire

First edition published © 2021 Catholics United for Life.

Cover by LUCAS Art & Design, Jenison, MI
Cover image: *Heart Icon* (Pixabay 2316451)

Nihil Obstat:
Rev. Christopher Beg, S.T.D., Ph.D.
Censor Deputatus

Imprimatur:
Very Rev. Daniel B. Carson
Vicar General and Moderator of the Curia
Sept. 8, 2021

The nihil obstat *and* imprimatur *are official declarations that a book or pamphlet is free of doctrinal or moral error. No implication is contained therein that those who have granted the nihil obstat and the imprimatur agree with the content, opinions or statements expressed therein.*

Sophia Institute Press
Box 5284, Manchester, NH 03108
1-800-888-9344
www.SophiaInstitute.com

Sophia Institute Press® is a registered trademark of Sophia Institute.

paperback ISBN 979-8-88911-582-3

ebook ISBN 979-8-88911-583-0

Library of Congress Control Number: 2025935921

First printing

Acknowledgments

My sincerest thanks to Barbara Meng, who read every word of this work and gave most helpful suggestions, and to Maria Blazevich for her many editorial corrections. I also thank all the people I have worked with in spiritual direction and in Courage, who have striven to overcome unchastity and have shared with me their struggles and triumphs. I am also indebted to the late Fr. Benedict Groeschel and Fr. John Harvey for their suggestions and their endorsements of this little book. Sincere thanks to my theological mentor, Dr. William E. May, for his endorsement. And thanks to my super proofreader, Olga Fairfax.

Contents

Achieving Chastity in an Unchaste World

INTRODUCTION

The Problem

WITH THE ADVENT of the internet and its huge number of pornographic websites, the pastoral problem of sexual struggles and addiction has skyrocketed. The advance of cable TV and streaming services has not helped matters. Many have developed addictions of varying intensity to pornography and other sexual activities such as masturbation, fornication, adultery, and homosexual acts.

People get into these things for various reasons: boredom, isolation, pleasure-seeking, or hurt. In many cases the sexual activity acts as a temporary alleviation from the pain one is experiencing, but sometimes it is just a seeking of pleasure. Sexual addictions are much like drug or other substance addictions, insofar as they provide a temporary high as a relief from sadness or boredom but also exact a price from the addict. In physical addictions the price is, most visibly, physical; in sexual addictions, the price is often psychological (and sometimes physical as well).

Of special note should be the physical changes in the brain which occur with the use of pornography. According to psychiatrist and faculty member at Harvard Medical School Kevin Majeres,

> When someone views pornography, he gets overstimulated by dopamine; so his brain destroys some dopamine receptors. This makes him feel depleted, so he goes back to pornography, but, having fewer dopamine receptors, this time it requires more to get the same dopamine thrill; but this causes his brain to destroy more receptors; so he feels an even greater need for pornography to stimulate him.[1]

Sexual addiction comes in many forms and in varying degrees. It ranges from the religious young man (or woman) trying to overcome masturbation, to a high-ranking religious leader being divulged as an exhibitionist, to the CEO of a large manufacturing company being

[1] Kevin Majeres, "The Science Behind Pornography," April 6, 2016, www.purityispossible.com/the-science-behind-pornography/.

caught leading a child pornography ring.[2] Whatever the degree, sexual addiction or even problems of sexual insobriety are a big challenge to the person of faith.

In helping scores of people over the past decades try to overcome bad sexual habits, I have found that the majority are not hard-core "sex addicts" like the CEO or the religious leader mentioned above. Most are simply people who have gotten into immoral sex and find it difficult to break free from the habit. Some have underlying psychological problems, such as a father wound, unresolved anger, or a gender identity deficit. Others have been the victims of sexual abuse. For all those cases, it seems that counseling with a good Christian therapist would be called for, and in some cases participation in a Sexaholics Anonymous group as well (which we will discuss later). For the more compulsive sex addict, therapy might also be necessary. This book is not aimed at taking the place of such therapy.

It is primarily aimed at the vast majority of men and women who struggle with a sex habit such as the

[2] See Patrick Carnes, *Out of the Shadows: Understanding Sexual Addiction* (Center City, MN: Hazelden, 2001), p. 71.

use of pornography, daily masturbation, or frequent fornication or other acting out. The issue addressed herein is how to use prayer and various methods from moral theology to overcome such habits. It's about the sex habit, not the more complex issues that may underlie the habit. Indeed, I believe some therapists, and ministers as well, could benefit from some of the ideas in this book as part of their particular approach, tailored to the individual they are counseling.

Ultimately, the question at hand is, how can we help people overcome such problems? What steps can those involved take to free themselves from the "sex drug"? The answer lies not just in exercising a rigid self-control, but in trying to harmonize moral behavior with human nature, in trying to change one's behavior in a way that is adapted to the psyche and what fulfills it. By accommodating both the truth about human sexuality and the nature of the human soul, and an overall healthy lifestyle, a person can find inner peace in living the Gospel, a peace that is lasting and joy-filled.

CHAPTER 1

Training the Sexual Appetite

SOME TIME AGO I was giving spiritual direction to a young man who struggled with unchaste thoughts and desires. He was praying a good deal each day and attending daily Mass. He had a reasonably balanced life, with some sports activities each week, and was happy in his job. Nonetheless, in this one area, he felt quite inadequate.

So, I explained to him the need to convert, rather than suppress, his appetite, as recommended by Aristotle, St. Thomas Aquinas, and Pope John Paul II (certainly a credible trio!). He was to present to his mind, repeatedly, the values he would gain by living chastely, things like "treating others as persons, not objects," "living by reason, not by his urges," and "upholding the sacredness of sex." I had him make a list of these reasons and encouraged him to read the list several times a day. He began to do this, and within a year, he told me he was over the struggle. He was able to live chastely without having to battle his sexual appetite. It had finally been trained, and it was not trying to move him in the direction of impure thoughts or acts. He had found chastity.

I have proposed similar routines to others, many of whom struggled with pornography, especially on the internet. A number of these people have indicated, after only a few months, that the routines were helping them a great deal.

It seems that all of this points to the fact that with a good deal of grace, and using the proper approach to the psyche, those struggling with addictions to pornography and unchaste thoughts and actions can be set free from their slavery to lust. How important is this emancipation? Very. Any addiction draws us away from our ultimate vocation, that of love, since only one who is free can give himself totally to another in love. Pope John Paul II spoke eloquently of the need for us to live out this love vocation:

> Man cannot live without love. He remains a being that is incomprehensible for himself, his life is senseless, if love is not revealed to him, if he does not encounter

> love, if he does not experience it and make it his own, if he does not participate intimately in it.[3]

It is only in love—love for God and for our neighbors—that we are fulfilled as persons.

The Goal: Chastity

To begin with, it's important to have the goal in mind. That goal must be real chastity. What exactly *is* the virtue of chastity? According to Thomas Aquinas and Aristotle, chastity is *the habitual moderation of the sexual appetite in accord with right reason.* In other words, it's bringing the sexual appetite consistently under reason.

Notice it is not just the regulation of *behavior,* which would be self-control, but of the very desires that lead to sexual behavior. Note too, the norm is "right" reason, i.e., reason in conformity with God's Eternal Law, not merely worldly reason, which sees

3 Pope John Paul II, *Redemptor hominis,* The Holy See, 1979, no. 10.

any sex which avoids unwanted pregnancy or disease as "reasonable."

Certainly, as a fruit of the Holy Spirit, chastity is not something a person can arrive at without considerable prayer and effort. The fruits of a tree appear last, and so it is with the Holy Spirit's fruits: they require a good deal of cultivation under the influence of God's grace.

Conversion

Are there any methods one can employ to effectively use the grace received from spiritual exercises to develop chastity? Yes, there are. A person begins by observing with Aristotle and Thomas Aquinas[4] that the sexual appetite seems to have a life of its own, and it listens not only to reason, but to the senses and the imagination as well. If I want to raise my hand, I direct it to move, and it moves. But, if my sexual appetite is attracted to something illicit, I must do more than tell it, "Forget it." It can be very persistent.

4 *Summa Theologica*, I, q 81 a 3; trans. Fathers of the English Dominican Province (New York: Benziger Bros., 1947), p. 1785.

St. Paul wrote,

> For I do not do the good I want, but the evil I do not want is what I do. … For I delight in the law of God, in my inmost self, but I see in my members another law at war with the law of my mind and making me captive to the law of sin which dwells in my members. Wretched man that I am! (Rom. 7:19, 23, 24)

This is the battle we have with the appetites, especially the sexual appetite.

Thus, one must find a way to "convince" his or her sexual appetite to obey reason and not the senses or the imagination. Alas, many who are addicted to sex are addicted to visual stimuli, especially pornography (senses), and sexual fantasies (imagination). We will consider how to deal with these elements below, but first, here is a general approach to converting the sexual appetite.

Political Dealings

Since there are competing voices for the control of the sexual appetite, it doesn't work for reason to deal with the appetite "despotically," i.e., simply saying "no" to the appetite's appeal, and when it asks why not, saying, "Because I said no." If it does, it will repress the appetite into the unconscious where it will wait for a chance to explode.[5] In a moment of weakness the appetite will indeed explode with an outburst of sexual activity. We see this in the person who contains himself/herself for several weeks but then goes on a spree and repeats this cycle over and over.

The intellect must deal "politically" with the appetite, setting forth the values which will be gained by living chastity, to make up for the value of the sexual pleasure which is sacrificed. One must, in a sense, *convince* his ("or her" understood) appetite that it will not make him happy to give in to it.

As Pope John Paul II put it,

> The promptings of carnal desire do not disappear merely because they are contained by willpower, although superficially they appear to do so; for them to disappear

[5] Karol Wojtyla (Pope John Paul II), *Love and Responsibility*, pp. 170, 198.

> completely a man must know "why" he is containing them. … We can speak of objectivization only when the will is confronted by a value which fully explains the necessity for containing impulses aroused by carnal desire and sensuality. Only as this value gradually takes possession of the mind and the will does the will become calm and free itself from a characteristic sense of loss.[6]

The person, then, must hammer away with reason to convert his heart to the truth. In the long run, we are more attracted to the truth than to pleasure. In fact, Jesus identified himself with the truth ("I am the way, the truth and the life," Jn. 14:6). Pleasure is a fleeting thing; truth lasts forever. It's not enough to know what is right and wrong. To survive in this world, chastity has got to be in one's blood. A person must be completely convinced, mind *and* heart.

While working to develop the virtue of chastity, the habit of turning away from unchaste activity, a person must have self-control to win battles with

6 *Love and Responsibility*, p. 198.

lustful thoughts when faced with them. What should you do when an impure image pops into your head unexpectedly? This actually happened to St. Catherine of Siena. Satan and his demons showed her figures of naked men and women sinning and invited her to join them. She repeated, "Jesus, Jesus, Jesus." Upon hearing that name, the demons left her alone. So that should be your first response: repeat the name *Jesus* over and over again. It's difficult to say a prayer like the Our Father or Hail Mary when you are in the heat of a battle like that, but repeating the Lord's name is easy and is often an effective strategy. Satan hates that name and is likely to leave when he hears it.

Secondly, you should immediately try to crowd out the thought with another colorful thought, such as a ball game, or a beautiful sunset, etc. In addition, you should take the advice of St. John Vianney to make a sign of the cross to drive away the temptation. In time you can make taking these measures reflex actions which you will carry out automatically when tempted.

Chapter 2

Chastity's Values

WHAT ARE SOME of these values (goods) of which a person can remind himself so as to alleviate any interior resentment and find peace in the chaste decision? I would propose at least six:

1. Sex is holy, not a plaything. It should never be trivialized.
2. Created in the image of God, I can live by reason, not just by urges (as the animals do).
3. Persons are to be loved, not merely used as objects of enjoyment.
4. I must not treat persons as objects, even in the mind, lest I become a user of persons in practice.
5. Unchaste activity destroys my most precious friendship, that with God, the source of all happiness.

6. Unchaste activity brings pleasure but not happiness.

Let's briefly discuss each of these.

The Sacredness and Beauty of Sexual Intimacy

One value retained by opting for chastity is that of upholding the sacredness of sex. It is so sacred that it belongs only in marriage. Virtually every decent person has a sense of the fact that sex is not some trivial act, but that it is quite different in importance from any other act. Few thoughtful people subscribe to the idea that promiscuity is virtuous. By living chastely, a person avoids trivializing sex as something merely recreational, so that if and when he does participate in it within marriage, he will experience its sublime dignity and transcendence.

An often-overlooked passage in Vatican II (*Gaudium et spes*) speaks of how the marital act both "expresses and perfects" conjugal love:

> This love is uniquely expressed and perfected through the act proper to marriage.

> Hence, the actions within marriage by which the couple are united intimately and chastely are noble and worthy. Expressed in a manner which is truly human, these actions signify and foster the mutual self-donation by which spouses enrich each other with a joyful and a ready mind. (GS 49b)

The Council speaks first of all of the marriage act expressing conjugal love; that is, it is a symbol of marital love or signifies it. The act means, "I love you in a conjugal way." This act also perfects and fosters this love, the mutual spousal self-donation; it enriches the couple. It enriches the spouses, not only through the joy of the act, but also because it is a celebration of their conjugal love, as the reception of Holy Communion celebrates our (conjugal) love with God. Each time bodily communion is effected, this love is declared and strengthened.

In a sense, the marital act celebrates the existence of conjugal love, proclaims it, and by perfecting it, in a sense *forms* the future of this love. It is not only a statement about the love that exists; it establishes the direction in which it will continue.

Pope John Paul II and his herald, Christopher West,[7] have done us a great service in proclaiming the beauty of sex as it was intended by the Creator, and the importance of what we do with our bodies. Without going into great detail, how can their work shed light on the sacredness and beauty of sex?

Pope John Paul II pointed out that "the body … and it alone, is capable of making visible what is invisible: the spiritual and the divine. It was created to transfer into the visible reality of the world the mystery hidden since time immemorial in God, and thus be a sign of it."[8] What is this mystery? The pope spoke of it later on when he commented on the communion of husband and wife and the fruit thereof, human life: "In this entire world there is not a more perfect, more complete image of God, Unity and

7 The following three paragraphs make use of the reasoning found in Christopher West's *Theology of the Body for Beginners* (Westchester, PA: Ascension Press, 2004), pp. 9–30.

8 Pope John Paul II, Theology of the Body talks (henceforth TB), February 20, 1980.

Community. There is no other human reality which corresponds more, humanly speaking, to that divine mystery."[9] One could say that a man and woman imitate God most profoundly at the natural level, when they express their love in such a way that it may overflow into new life in the marriage act, for this is what God did at creation.

"Man became the image and likeness of God not only through his humanity," said the pope, "but also through the communion of persons which man and woman form right from the beginning." Together, in communion, they become "an image of an inscrutable divine communion of persons."[10] In addition, the union of husband and wife in marriage is, as St. Paul proclaimed (Eph. 5:32), a sacrament, a sacred sign of Christ and His Church. In other words, this union and its symbolic act are sacramental, just as our communion with God is sacramental.

In fact, Pope John Paul II declared that "the Eucharist ... is the sacrament of the Bridegroom and of

[9] TB, December 30, 1981.

[10] TB, November 14, 1979.

the Bride." He said that Christ, "in instituting the Eucharist ... wished to express the relationship between man and woman, between what is 'feminine' and what is 'masculine.'"[11] It is based on this that Christopher West aptly places Christ's Eucharistic words in the mouths of spouses, "This is my body, given for you."[12]

What happens when people use this sacred language symbolic of divine love and creativity for mere pleasure, and compulsive pleasure at that? They drag their very nobility through the mud. They draw mankind down from the threshold of divinity to the realm of animality. They take what is holy and treat it as something trivial and diminish themselves in the process.[13]

[11] Pope John Paul II, *Mulieris dignitatem*, no. 26. See Christopher West, *Theology of the Body for Beginners*, p. 9.

[12] Ibid., for example, p. 10.

[13] I believe that this sort of "high sexology" of St. John Paul II and Christopher West is an excellent antidote to the "low sexology" spawned by the sexual revolution. The work of Mr. West, despite its occasional diversions into hyperbole, is key for the rehabilitation of sex as truly sacramental, in that it makes more readily available and understandable the thought of the pope. For

Human Dignity

A further value which follows closely on the previous one is that by opting for chastity, one will be living up to his or her own human dignity as a person created in the image and likeness of God. As such, we are empowered to live by reason, rather than merely being controlled by urges and impulses (as are animals). Pope John Paul II spoke of the "freedom of the gift" that their nakedness without shame implied. Referring to Vatican II, the pope recalled the pivotal passage from *Gaudium et spes* (24),

> Indeed, the Lord Jesus, when He prayed to the Father "that all may be one … as we are one" (John 17:21-22), opened up vistas closed to human reason, for He implied a certain likeness between the union of the divine Persons, and the unity of God's sons in truth and charity. This likeness reveals that man, who is the only creature on earth which God willed for itself, cannot fully find himself except through a sincere gift of himself.

---

those who need more convincing, I recommend West's courses on the Theology of the Body, available at www.christopherwest.com/store.asp.

The pope declared that in order for one to give himself to another, he must have mastery of himself, "self-control." So, to find himself, man must be able to control himself, not in some arbitrary way, but according to reason. To have true self-control, in the image of God, is to live by reason. Reason, as we saw above, reveals to us that sex is something sacred and beautiful, and its trivialization is tragic.

Loving, Not Using, Persons

When a person has sex with another outside of marriage, there is a natural tendency to see the other as an object of enjoyment, rather than as an object of love. Pope John Paul II, in his analysis of Genesis, pointed out the meaning of the shame which came about after Original Sin. The fact that Adam and Eve were naked without shame before the Fall indicates that they had the full vision of each other as God saw them.

> Seeing each other, as if through the very mystery of creation, man and woman see each other even more fully and distinctly than through the sense of sight itself, that is,

> through the eyes of the body. They see and know each other, in fact, with all the peace of the interior gaze, which creates precisely the fullness of the intimacy of persons.[14]

This vision was not exploitive, but loving.

With the Fall came a more superficial vision, in which exterior values dominated over interior; the response was to the body rather than to the person. This is the reason for the post-Fall shame. "Shame is a tendency," wrote the Holy Father, "uniquely characteristic of the human person, to conceal sexual values sufficiently to prevent them from obscuring the value of person as such."[15]

With redemption, we are called to:

> Rediscover, nay more, realize the nuptial meaning of the body and to express in this way the interior freedom of the gift, that is, of that spiritual state and that spiritual power which are derived from mastery of the lust of the flesh. . . .

[14] TB, January 2, 1980.

[15] *Love and Responsibility*, p. 187.

> Christ's words bear witness that the original power (therefore also the grace) of the mystery of creation becomes for each of them power (that is, grace) of the mystery of redemption.[16]

The "new man" can come forth as the *ethos* (the ethical pattern) of the redemption of the body "dominates the lust of the flesh and the whole man of lust. Redemption contains the imperative of self-control, the necessity of immediate continence and habitual temperance."[17]

The redeemed new man is one who loves others rather than uses them. This temperance with regard to sex is, of course, chastity. The connection between chastity and love comes out of the personalistic norm: The person is a good towards which the only proper and adequate attitude is love.[18] Thus, said St. John Paul II,

[16] TB, October 29, 1980.

[17] TB, December 3, 1980.

[18] *Love and Responsibility*, p. 41. Stated negatively, the personalist norm is: The person is the kind of good which does not admit of use and cannot be treated as an object of use (and as such the means to an end).

> The virtue of chastity, whose function it is to free love from utilitarian attitudes, must control not only sensuality and carnal concupiscence, as such, but—perhaps more important—those centers deep within the human being in which the utilitarian attitude is hatched and grows.... To be chaste means to have a "transparent" attitude to a person of the other sex—*chastity means just that—the inner "transparency"* without which love is not itself, for it cannot be itself until the desire to "enjoy" is subordinated to a readiness to show loving kindness in every situation.[19]

One need not be an ethicist to realize that it is wrong to exploit people, sexually or otherwise. Even visual exploitation is wrong, since exploiting someone in the mind will result in exploiting them in practice.

Destroying Our Most Precious Friendship

Certainly unchaste activity destroys our relationship with God (until we are able to restore it by sincere

[19] *Love and Responsibility*, p. 170.

repentance and the Sacrament of Reconciliation). Jesus Himself spoke of the evil of fornication:

> From within, out of the heart of man, come evil thoughts, *fornication*, theft, murder, adultery, coveting, wickedness, deceit, licentiousness, envy. ... All these evil things come from within, and they defile a man.[20] (emphasis added)

St. Paul had something similar to say:

> Do you not know that the unjust will not inherit the kingdom of God? Do not be deceived; neither *fornicators* nor idolaters nor adulterers nor boy prostitutes nor sodomites nor thieves nor the greedy nor drunkards nor slanderers nor robbers will inherit the kingdom of God.[21] (emphasis added)

Being excluded from the Kingdom is the result of persisting in sin which destroys our relationship with

[20] Mark 7:21-23; see also Matt. 15:19, 20.

[21] 1 Cor. 6:9, New American Bible (New York: Catholic Book Publishing Co., 1991); see also Gal. 5:19-21.

God. (Of course, repentance and reconciliation are always possible in this life, for those who sincerely seek them.)

Why is this so? Most notably, in light of the arguments given above with regard to the very sacredness and beauty of sex, wherein man most closely approaches the action of God at the natural level, because sex signifies a matrimonial covenant and an openness to new life. Neither is ordinarily present in fornication.

The immorality of *adultery* is clearly stated in the Ten Commandments. In addition to the reasons given for fornication's immorality, adultery has the added evil of violating the fidelity of marriage.

It is not only non-marital sexual intercourse which is sinful. All deliberate non-marital sexual arousal is sinful. Thomas Aquinas wrote:

> Since fornication is a mortal sin, and much more so the other kinds of lust, it follows that in such like sins not only consent to the act but also consent to the pleasure is a mortal sin. Consequently when … kisses

> and caresses are done for this delight, it follows that they are mortal sins.[22]

The Church addresses this same issue in the *Catechism of the Catholic Church* as well: "Sexual pleasure is morally disordered when sought for itself, isolated from its procreative and unitive purposes" (CCC 2351). The unitive purpose implies the celebration of the existing marital love covenant. In other words, sexual pleasure may be sought only in marriage.

There are some who have been addicted to *foreplay* even if they have avoided fornication. Why is this wrong? Because it too trivializes sex by using sexual arousal as mere recreation, rather than as a noble introduction to marital union.

Pornography is another abuse of sex. It is an implicit statement that sex is recreational and women (or men) are objects of pleasure. Although people don't go into pornography with these lies in mind, but often do so just for the pleasure involved, they come out branded with these attitudes, which are so

22 *Summa Theologica*, II-II, q 154 a 4.

destructive. It is no wonder that the *Catechism of the Catholic Church* teaches that "[pornography] is a grave offense" (CCC 2354).

Masturbation is another serious sin. Why? Because it not only degrades sex by using it for mere pleasure, but also turns a person in on himself in the very act which is meant to signify and perfect communion with a spouse. C. S. Lewis put it well:

> For me the real evil of masturbation would be that it takes an appetite which, in lawful use, leads the individual out of himself to complete (and correct) his own personality in that of another (and finally in children and even grandchildren) and turns it back, sends it back into the prison of himself, there to keep a harem of imaginary brides. And this harem, once admitted, works against his ever getting out and really uniting with a real woman. For the harem is always accessible, always subservient, calls for no sacrifices or adjustments, and can be endowed with

> erotic and psychological attractions which no real woman can rival.[23]

The Church has spoken clearly of the immorality of *masturbation* (CCC 2352):

> "Both the Magisterium of the Church, in the course of a constant tradition, and the moral sense of the faithful have been in no doubt and have firmly maintained that masturbation is an intrinsically and gravely disordered action." (CDF, *Persona humana 9*) "The deliberate use of the sexual faculty, for whatever reason, outside of marriage is essentially contrary to its purpose." For here sexual pleasure is sought outside of "the sexual relationship which is demanded by the moral order and in which the total meaning of mutual self-giving and human procreation in the context of true love is achieved."

[23] Leanne Payne, *The Broken Image* (Wheaton, IL: Crossway Books, 1981), p. 91. The complete text is found in: Letter to a Mr. Masson (March 6, 1956), Wade Collection, Wheaton College, Wheaton, IL.

However, as we shall see later, the Church in this same section cautions us to evaluate carefully subjective guilt in regard to masturbation.

Homosexual activity is another violation of the sexual order which is serious matter. St. Paul said in 1 Corinthians (6:9ff.),

> Do not be deceived; neither fornicators nor idolaters nor adulterers nor boy prostitutes nor sodomites [the Greek here is *arseno-koites*, combining the two words *arsén*, meaning male, and *koité*, meaning bed. Thus, a more literal translation would be "men bedding men"], nor thieves nor the greedy nor drunkards nor slanderers nor robbers will inherit the kingdom of God.

The Church has confirmed this in the *Catechism* (CCC 2357):

> Basing itself on Sacred Scripture, which presents homosexual acts as acts of grave depravity, tradition has always declared that "homosexual acts are intrinsically disordered." They are contrary to the

> natural law. They close the sexual act to the gift of life. They do not proceed from a genuine affective and sexual complementarity. Under no circumstances can they be approved.

While the Church is clear in proclaiming *homosexual acts* as seriously sinful, she also wishes us to show respect and compassion to those who suffer with this condition:

> They must be accepted with respect, compassion, and sensitivity. Every sign of unjust discrimination in their regard should be avoided. These persons are called to fulfill God's will in their lives and, if they are Christians, to unite to the sacrifice of the Lord's Cross the difficulties they may encounter from their condition. (CCC 2358)

The Theology of the Body should make it clear that homosexual acts contain none of the noble elements which make conjugal union man's most God-like natural act.

All of these sins involving the misuse of sex are serious matter. The Church taught in 1975, "The moral order of sexuality involves such high values of human life that every direct violation of this order is objectively serious."[24]

This, it seems, covers all those violations of chastity which lend themselves to addiction. Each has the potential, if done with sufficient reflection and full consent of the will, to destroy one's relationship with God. This is a huge price to pay for a few moments of pleasure.

Pleasure, Not Happiness

Finally, unchaste activity may provide pleasure, but this is not what brings us happiness as persons. Only love—love of God and love of neighbor—will make us happy. Unchaste activity qualifies for neither. One need only compare the lives of the saints to the lives of debauchers. The latter often had smiles on their faces, but the former glowed.

[24] *Declaration on Sexual Ethics*, henceforth, *DSE*, Congregation for the Doctrine of the Faith, 1975, para. 10.

Changing the Heart

As we saw in the opening story of the young man struggling with chastity, by reminding oneself of these values over and over a person can, in a sense, graft reason onto the appetite, to the point that the appetite in time will appear to participate in reason. The values of chastity must be "objectivized," internalized, such that the will is "constantly confronted by a value which fully explains the necessity for containing impulses aroused by carnal desire and sensuality. Only as this value takes possession of the mind and will does the will become calm and free itself from a characteristic sense of loss."[25] In other words, one must repeatedly recall the truth about sex and his or her own happiness, until the appetite in a sense "gives up" and surrenders to reason. Only when this happens is the appetite in conformity with the mind, and does one arrive at the peace of chastity. Another way of putting this is, it's not enough to convert one's mind; he must convert his heart as well.[26]

25 *Love and Responsibility*, p. 198.

26 Much of the above text, beginning with the subtitle, "The Goal: Chastity," is taken almost word for word from the author's book, *Christian Dating in a*

Those who have struggled with sexual addictions know very well that it doesn't work to try to avoid thinking about these things, hoping the temptations will go away. They won't. One must think about the positive values of chastity often. It's not enough to remind oneself of these values only when tempted. A person needs to call them to mind several times a day and really meditate on them.

Why is this effective? Because, as we mentioned earlier, in the long run we are more attracted to truth than to pleasure. But we must penetrate the thick skin of pleasure with the truth before truth can take hold of our whole being.

It is only when the heart, the emotions themselves, have been converted by reason that the person will experience true peace with regard to sexual matters. Self-control, whereby one struggles and wins, is not a full virtue, as St. Thomas taught. Chastity enables one to avoid sexual sins without a struggle, and it is attainable.

Godless World, (Manchester, NH: Sophia Institute Press, 2016), 81-87.

✠ ✠ ✠

This "converting the appetite" is really the key to arriving at the peace of chastity, something that many in our world doubt can even happen. Some might say, "It can't be that easy!" bringing to mind the complaint of Naaman who doubted he could be healed just by washing seven times in the Jordan (2 Kings 5:1-14).

However, it's really *not* so easy. Many compose a card with all the reasons why they should be chaste and read it for a few weeks, and then for one reason or another, they let it slide. Perhaps they were expecting quicker results (it can take a year or more) or they lost the card and failed to compose another. Or, perhaps they have been struggling with this so long, they don't really believe they can change.

But people *do* change, and dramatically so. However, it takes a good deal of motivation and perseverance in reading the "values" of chastity and letting the truth permeate one's whole being, mind, and heart. If it took two or three years of reading the benefits of chastity three or four times a day (requiring perhaps three minutes a day), would it be worth it?

Of course, the Christian has much more than just a psychological technique to help him overcome sexual insobriety. He has the ability to benefit from grace, the grace that all people need to live virtuous lives. And, there are any number of other aids for the Christian striving to move from vice to virtue. We will consider these in the next chapter.

It should be noted as well, that chastity is not just about sex, but it should be part of a whole Christian lifestyle, which is balanced, realistic about what the world can offer, and built on the virtue of prudence. These things will be addressed in subsequent chapters.

CHAPTER 3

Get Help

Grace

The first help a believer should seek is grace. St. Augustine said, “The law was given that we might seek grace. Grace was given that we might keep the law.” Prayer opens us to the entire life of grace. Christians can meditate on the life of Christ as one of the most powerful types of prayer. Catholics can do this by meditation on the mysteries of the Rosary,[27] but all Christians can meditate on the Scriptures. This is done by reading a passage and then closing one’s eyes and reflecting on what was read.

One young man told me he had struggled with an addiction to homosexual activity for many years, and then masturbation for several years more. When one day he began to pray the Divine Mercy Chaplet

[27] For meditations on the mysteries which you may download, go to www.cdn.shopify.com/s/files/1/0012/8506/2743/files/Wmpm21.pdf?v=1616875336.

(after years of prayer), all of a sudden he was given the grace of chastity. Prayer is essential for chastity, and indeed, for all the fruits of the Holy Spirit.

To be sure, the Divine Mercy Chaplet was the final piece in a mosaic of prayer for the man just mentioned. It usually takes a good deal of time to arrive at chastity. However long it takes, grace is essential for it to happen. As noted earlier, the fruits are generally the last thing to appear on a tree, and it is no different with the fruit of chastity. One must persevere in prayer, and make a constant effort to overcome sexual sins, and the peace of chastity will come.

And prayer here is not just something one does until he is healed. It's a way of life for the Christian. Many have discovered the hard way that when they stopped praying, having achieved the goal of chastity, lust comes roaring back. Prayer is not a temporary medicine for sin, but the basic spiritual food of every Christian. Even if we were to live in perfect chastity for the rest of our lives, it would mean very little if we did not have a strong relationship with God through prayer. Prayer is the way to true happiness, and every follower of Christ should know that. Prayer draws us close to the Lord in love, which is essential to our being saved. It's far more than a remedy for lust.

And, as St. John Vianney said, "The more you pray, the more you want to pray." Alas, the opposite is true as well: the less you pray, the less you want to pray. A person who struggles with sexual addiction—or any addiction—should commit to ten or fifteen minutes of prayer daily and then try to increase that commitment every six months or so. The commitment to pray is the first miracle in the life of a Christian, as St. Augustine said. Once that commitment is made and kept for a year, adding to it is relatively easy.

The beautiful thing about prayer is that once a person makes it a habit, he begins to see the results of prayer and becomes highly motivated to keep going. One woman commented about her discovery of prayer and all that flowed from it, "I am never going back to my old ways. I've found it and I'm never going to let go."

Mother Teresa of Calcutta said,

> Love to pray. Feel often during the day the need for prayer and take the trouble to pray. Prayer enlarges the heart until it is

> capable of containing God's gift of Himself. Ask and seek, and your heart will grow big enough to receive Him and keep Him as your own.

There are, of course, other sources of grace besides prayer. In a Catholic context, the Mass is the highest source of grace, the "source and summit of the Christian life," as Vatican II put it.[28] Catholics have the opportunity to attend Mass not only on Sunday, but on weekdays as well. This is a most powerful source of grace. Most of the Catholics I know who have been set free from lust are attending Mass every day. Certainly the sacraments, especially the sacrament of Penance and Reconciliation[29] and that of the Eucharist, are also great sources of grace.

In addition to these things, the daily reading of Sacred Scripture and books on the saints[30] and their writings is an invaluable source of inspiration to

28 *Lumen gentium*, no. 11.

29 See a card ("A Brief Guide to Confession") on how to confess at www.cfalive.com.

30 For a list of recommended books ("A Guide to Spiritual Reading for Adults"), see www.cfalive.com.

continue on the journey toward holiness. And it *is* holiness that one needs to be free of sexual addiction, and even more so for salvation.

Fasting for Chastity?

Thomas Aquinas taught that one of the purposes of fasting was

> In order to bridle the lusts of the flesh, wherefore the Apostle says (2 Cor. 6:5, 6): "In fasting, in chastity," since fasting is the guardian of chastity. For, according to Jerome, "Venus is cold when Ceres and Bacchus are not there," that is to say, lust is cooled by abstinence in meat and drink. … The same is declared by Augustine in a sermon, "Fasting cleanses the soul, raises the mind, subjects one's flesh to the spirit … scatters the clouds of concupiscence, quenches the fire of lust, kindles the true light of chastity."[31]

So, if a person is eating rich foods and drinking exotic beverages on a regular basis, this would make it that

[31] *Summa Theologica*, II-IIae, q 147, a 1.

much harder to advance in chastity. Thomas Aquinas taught that fasting and self-denial are required by Christianity,[32] and the neglect of these will make pursuing chastity difficult.

In addition, of course, excessive drinking makes one far more vulnerable to sexual sins. This is so because becoming inebriated lowers one's moral powers.

Mentors

Another source of help would be to work with a mentor or spiritual director. This should be a priest or minister, or devout psychologist or other layperson who knows the spiritual life and has some understanding of sexual addictions. One might contact such a person weekly by phone and perhaps monthly in person. In some cases, phone contact might be the only practical possibility because of a lack of proximity, and that can work fine. What one must do is to share with the mentor exactly what he has done with regard to this addiction and how he has pursued prayer and other spiritual practices to

[32] Luke 5:35; Matt. 16:24. Also, Thomas Aquinas wrote, "Fasting in general is a matter of precept of the natural law" (*Summa Theologica*, II-IIae, q 147 a 3).

strengthen himself since their last contact. If progress is to be made, the person must candidly tell the mentor everything that is pertinent.

I once mentored a young man who was struggling with pornography addiction. At one point he began to be very vague and evasive. I knew that this young man would not continue with me, and indeed, he did not. If a person is to make his way out of this slavery, he must be absolutely committed to staying with his mentor (if the mentor is helping), until the addiction is overcome.

Counseling

As I mentioned in the introduction, some may need therapy to overcome their sexual addiction. I would recommend a well-formed Christian therapist, since many seculars might be hard-pressed to understand why anyone would want to stop non-marital sexual activity. Even some Christian therapists might see nothing wrong with masturbation. And, of course, regardless of the therapist's religious affiliation, some are better than others. It is ultimately up to the person seeking help to decide after a certain time if the therapist is helping. If not, he should feel free to seek another therapist.

A New Psychological Approach[33]

New psychological theories[34] propose that our personality is made up of parts and that each of us has many parts, each with their own individual personality. Humans are complex beings, and it is helpful to know that when we have an addiction to pornography, masturbation, or other sexual practices, it is not all of us that is addicted but rather a part of us. The part that has the unwanted desire controls our actions, but only some of the time. Although the addiction can be overwhelming and feel like it is in total control some of the time, knowing it is only a segment of who we are can be reassuring.

So, how can you work with the addictive part is the question. You might like to just cut it out and be rid of this element of your personality, but the more you reject and fight it, the more tenacious it seems to be. So, the way to deal with the addicted part is to become familiar with it, to discover what is behind it.

[33] This section was contributed by mental health therapist Patricia Adams, LCPC, NCC, EMDR certified, Rockville, MD.

[34] Schwartz, R.C., & Falconer, R.R., *Many Minds, One Self: Evidence for a Radical Shift in Paradigm* (Trailhead Publications, 2017).

It was not created out of nothing; it has a purpose, and it is in some way trying to meet a need or protect you.

Even though many people become sexually addicted simply because of the pleasure involved, it may have to do with something deeper in some cases. It may be that one is addicted to pornography or masturbation for one of the following reasons:

1. Feeling powerless with girls, women, or mother,[35] or curiosity about having power over women.
2. Being unable to win the affection of a woman in the past. It could have been being awkward as a teen or bullied by girls or women.
3. Feeling unloved by parents, especially by a mother who may have been unavailable for a close connection with the person in childhood.
4. Peer pressure regarding having a woman; being ridiculed for a lack of self-confidence with members of the opposite sex.

[35] We focus more on men dealing with this issue because 70 percent of pornography users are men, but all of this could apply to the other 30 percent of pornography users, women.

5. Sexual abuse, leading to regarding sex lightly. The part mimics what it saw others do; if sexual abuse helped them to feel close to another then this is a coping mechanism for loneliness.
6. Normal curiosity of young people.[36]

Many of these mistaken ideas were formed at a younger age, and reflect a degree of immaturity.

So, our troublesome part is locked in a prison, exiled from the rest of our personality with a distorted belief. Our task is to find that exiled part that has been locked away and release it from the wounds that seem permanent. How do we find these elements and release them from the pain of rejection, distortion, or self-deception?

The best way is to look closely at this part of you in prayer. Ask for the light to discover exactly what it is. As you get to know this part which may be known through an image, an emotion, thought, memory, or

[36] This can go very badly when they experiment and find the rush of dopamine very intoxicating and do not have a trusted adult to help them understand what is happening in their brain that draws them into deeper and darker encounters. (See www.intellectualtakeout.org/blog/harvard-scientist-explains-what-porn-does-your-brain/.)

feeling in your body, just go inside and listen. Have curiosity and compassion for this part of you and notice how it wants to communicate with you. As you get more information, and this part begins to feel understood, it begins to soften and change. The part will begin to have conversations or send images in a way that will let you know and understand the wound or emotion that needs to be healed. You may have to sit with uncomfortable feelings such as worthlessness, guilt, loneliness, anger, or sadness. As you sit with these feelings, hold onto the Blessed Mother and Jesus and breathe. You may need help from a professional to find just what these feelings are or if they are overwhelming. You should reach out for help as a way of supporting you and this part in healing.

Healing includes praying for this part and asking for the grace of understanding and forgiveness for those who may have hurt this aspect of your personhood. Take this part with you to Mass and Communion. Take this part and any wounded parts you discover to Mary with her power of unconditional love. Take this part to Jesus and notice how it begins to change, soften, lose power, and become more compliant. As you have more compassion and understanding for the segment of you that has caused the addiction, you can help meet its needs in more authentic and emotionally healthy ways. Once you get to know this part, remember to check in on it and help it to find a safe and secure place to be tucked into.

Support Groups

Another source of great help is to attend a support group such as Sexaholics Anonymous.[37] This group is quite compatible with Christianity, insofar as their criterion for sobriety is: no sexual activity except with a spouse in a true marriage. Other support groups for sexual addictions seem to leave the goal entirely to the individual. It may not be easy to strive for a truly Christian goal while your peers are working toward a much lesser goal.

Courage is the Catholic support group for those dealing with same-sex attractions who wish to live biblical chastity.[38] There are a number of other orthodox Christian support groups under

37 www.sa.org for local meetings. For phone or online Zoom meetings go to www.saphonemeeting.org/index.html.

38 www.couragerc.net.

Protestant leadership. One such group is Regeneration Ministries.[39]

Get a Life

Having worked with scores of people struggling with sexual addiction over the years, I have found one pattern which seems to emerge over and over again: namely, boredom with life. Most people in this predicament worked at their jobs daily but had rather mundane lives evenings and on weekends. They had few or no enjoyable activities in their lives on a regular basis. I had to urge them to plan some fun every week.

The reason for this is not obscure. The human psyche needs some stimulation periodically to feel healthy. If we don't take care of this need, the mind will become desperate for stimulation and seek it in the wrong places. Destructive mental stimulation becomes a drug that can be found by a visit to the internet, a quick fix for the mind.

People striving to overcome sex addiction must find some enjoyable activity such as a sport or game,

[39] www.regenerationministries.org.

or some creative activity which they will look forward to each week. It is especially helpful if what they choose involves at least one other person. Even the reading of a fascinating book or watching a great movie would suffice. It must be something that will lift the mind out of what the French call *ennui*, that annoying boredom that comes with a lackluster life.

Exercise can not only be a good stimulant for the mind, but it also dampens the appetite for unchaste behavior. Anyone who has exercised vigorously for an hour or two knows that his interest in illicit sexual activity is lower after exercising than before.

The person who fails to integrate healthy fun into his life becomes an easy prey for not only sexual addiction, but for substance abuse and love addiction as well. It is a dangerous state to be in.

A young woman came to me for counseling once because she was having a terrible time with her boyfriend. He often tried to manipulate her and they had ugly arguments rather frequently. She said she had broken up with him several times before, but after a week or two she would call him and they would get back together. She knew he wasn't right for her, but she had a hard time letting go. I asked her if she had any fun in her life and she replied no, her work schedule didn't permit it.

"It's no wonder you keep going through this cycle," I told her. "You are so bored with your life that after you have broken up with Marvin for a couple of weeks, you call him for a little excitement. You need to consider finding a new job so that you will have time to have some real fun every week."

She got a new job, and she began to have some fun. Shortly thereafter, she broke up with Marvin for the last time. Some months later she met a very good man and eventually married him.

Having enjoyable activities to anticipate each week is not a luxury, nor is it pampering oneself; it is a basic need. Pursuing this is not self-indulgence but, analogous to eating or sleeping enough, an acknowledgment of our own human neediness. It is part of the virtue of humility.

Certainly, doing enjoyable things can be overdone, as when a person has to play his sport five times a week to the neglect of his duties. This is going beyond needs to irrational desires.

Sometimes one's boredom is more than just lack of healthy stimulation. It can be due to a complete lack of purpose in life. Certainly, knowing one's faith and reading about how the saints lived it is a great beginning to overcoming this lack in one's life. Knowing one's purpose, both eternal and temporal, and pursuing it constitute a good antidote to general boredom.

Healthy, non-possessive friendships are another antidote to sexual addiction. Getting together with a friend or two weekly or so, to watch a game or just have a drink and talk about life, can be very worthwhile.

Chapter 4

Love Addiction

THE WOMAN IN the previous story was suffering not only from boredom, but from love addiction as well. The two were feeding each other. Love addiction can often lead to unchastity, if not to a habit of lust. It can also lead to marrying the wrong person—or persons!

The problem arises when an individual meets someone he likes, and he immediately thinks of this person as a potential spouse. Of course, such thoughts are fairly natural when you meet someone new, but what a person does with them is the key. Some dismiss them for the first nine months or so, until they really get to know the person. Only then do they begin to really allow their emotions to develop more strongly, but not before. This is very smart.

The sad thing is that others, many others, will really believe these premature thoughts and begin to obsess over the person. They blow the relationship all out of proportion and interiorly commit to the other person. The trouble with this is a) This passion in the heart often leads to passionate activity, including sexual activity, even if there is a commitment to chastity; and b) It sets a person up to make a terrible mistake by marrying someone he doesn't really know.

One young college woman was so committed to chastity that she developed into an excellent speaker on the subject. She was invited to speak at various schools and convocations on chastity. Then she met a man who she thought was the man of her dreams. Right from the beginning she let her heart run wild over him. He seemed to be a good Catholic and interested in the very sort of family life she wanted. She would tell family and friends, "We are so in love. We just can't get enough of each other." They acted as if they had discovered something no one else ever experienced.

As a feeling, that's okay, but her mistake was to believe it, to try to live it out, to try to consume this man and be consumed by him emotionally. She had little time for her friends, and barely enough time for her studies. They were so filled with passion when they got together, that one night her passion, combined with his old ways of dealing with women, overcame her commitment to chastity. As it turned out, that night she got pregnant. Needless to say her life became complicated very quickly. And her chastity talks ended.

How should she have proceeded with her new love? Enjoy the strong feelings, but realize they are all out of proportion to reality. No human being can satisfy that overpowering *eros* which masquerades as a god.[40] The purpose of this emotional high is solely to inspire a couple to overcome inertia and make the commitment to marry when the time is right. To cultivate it and give in to it at any other time is a recipe for disaster.

If it doesn't lead to unchastity, it could lead to a huge marriage mistake. In this case the person totally commits his heart to his latest love after two months or less of dating. In some cases, the man will propose after this outrageously short time and the woman will say yes. They come to me and explain that everything

40 "An intoxicated and undisciplined *eros*, then, is not an ascent in ecstasy towards the Divine, but a fall, a degradation of man. Evidently, *eros* needs to be disciplined and purified if it is to provide not just fleeting pleasure, but a certain foretaste of the pinnacle of our existence, of that beatitude for which our whole being yearns." From Pope Benedict XVI, *Deus caritas est,* no. 4. See also no. 5.

is in place. They agree on religion, on chastity, on natural birth regulation in marriage, on the number of children they want to have. "Everything is right," they say. "Why wait?"

I tell them why. "Because you don't really know each other. That's a factor here too. It's no doubt refreshing to find someone with whom you have so much in common, and to actually *like* this person, but it's not enough." How many, many couples have met either through computer dating or other means and after having checked off all the key moral questions, rushed into marriage, only to find out that there were a number of interpersonal items they had overlooked.

I prepared one such couple for marriage. The groom had proposed ever-so-romantically after two months. The woman, a devout Catholic, was impressed with his faith and his apparent maturity (anyone can be mature for two months). She said yes, and four months later they were married. It was not even a year later when he wanted out of the marriage. It was a disaster. They realized they hadn't gotten to know each other (the understatement of the year!). A sad divorce followed.

Both men and women must realize that it takes time to get to know someone before marriage, even if some of the most important criteria are met. Have there been any studies done to see what length of courtship produces good results in marriage? I know of at least one. In the mid-eighties, researchers at Kansas State University studied marital satisfaction in relation to time of courtship. The results? "Couples who had dated for more than two years scored consistently high on marital satisfaction, while couples who had dated for shorter periods scored in a wide range from very high to very low."[41]

This is why I encourage couples to never give way to passionate feelings until they have dated nine months to a year. And even then, one must subject these feelings to reasonable limits. Even in marriage, you cannot expect to have all your emotional needs met by your spouse. As Bishop Fulton Sheen used to say, "Every man (woman) promises what only God

[41] Kelly Grover et al., "Mate Selection Processes and Marital Satisfaction," *Family Relations*, Vol. 34, 1985, pp. 383-386. As found in Neil Clark Warren, *Finding the Love of Your Life* (New York: Simon and Schuster, 1992), p. 9.

can give." Indeed, even with God, we will not be somehow dissolved into Him in the Kingdom, but are in an eternal exchange of love between distinct persons. Pope John Paul II stated,

> This intimacy—with all its subjective intensity—will not absorb man's personal subjectivity, but rather will make it stand out to an incomparably greater and fuller extent. … Those who participate in the future world, that is, in perfect communion with the living God, will enjoy a perfectly mature subjectivity.[42]

Prior to nine months, lovers should simply enjoy the feelings, but tell themselves, "This is nice, but it doesn't mean much at this point. We need to take our time."

One woman came to me for spiritual guidance and told me of her latest love, whom she had met just a few months before. She said, "Things seem to be going well. I suppose it's unlikely, based on past experience, that this will end in marriage, but I am keeping an open mind." In other words, she was not

[42] TB, December 9 and 16, 1981.

rushing her heart to the altar after just a few months, since she had been very much in love before that time and it hadn't worked out. In fact, that relationship did work out, but the wedding was over a year away.

Love addiction is a huge problem in our "instant gratification" culture, and is related to sex addiction, to the extent that there is actually a support group with chapters throughout the world, entitled "Sex and Love Addicts Anonymous." They identify some of the symptoms of being "Sex and Love Addicted" as becoming "sexually involved with and/or emotionally attached to people without knowing them," and returning to "painful, destructive relationships."[43]

The point of all this is that you can't let your passions go wild after only a short time of knowing someone and expect to control yourself sexually. It's virtually impossible. But, even if you could exercise a will of steel while allowing your emotions to prematurely take over, you still run the terrible risk of doing something stupid, like getting married to someone without really knowing him or her.

[43] See www.slaafws.org.

CHAPTER 5

Cleansing the Mind

WE CAN SIN sexually not only with our bodies, but with our minds as well. Jesus taught, "I say to you that every one who looks at a woman lustfully has already committed adultery with her in his heart" (Matt. 5:28). Thus, it is essential that we keep our minds clean of impure thoughts.

Get Rid of Pornography

One fellow who struggled with pornography told me he went to confession often so as to be able to go to Communion. I asked him whether the priests had told him he must get rid of any pornographic materials he had, and he replied no. I told him he needed to do that to have a firm purpose of amendment. There is simply no way a person can be reconciled to God while hanging on to pornographic materials. Anyone who has such things must throw them all in the trash, and confessors need to tell penitents as much. If a person has these images stored in his computer, he needs to erase them all as well.

Unfortunately, with such easy access to pornography on the internet, one must do more than just discard all pornography. He must doctor his internet browser so that he will not be able to go to pornographic sites. Some have signed up with an internet service provider which carefully monitors websites and blocks access to pornographic ones. If a person has a difficulty in this area, these are well worth it. To find a good pornography blocker, type in "Best porn blockers" and choose from those that come up.

Bishop Fulton Sheen told the story of a young man in college whose roommate hung pornographic pictures on his wall in their small dorm room. He asked Sheen what he could do. Sheen suggested he hang a large picture of Christ crucified on his wall. He did, and it wasn't long before the roommate's pornography came down. Taking a cue from this, I have suggested to a number of men that they tape a small picture of the crucified Christ on their computer monitor. When they look at this, they find it much harder to pursue internet pornography.

Purify the Mind

If a person has been using impure images or engaging in immoral sexual behavior for some time, he will most likely have to struggle with impure images even after he has given up his disordered behavior. How does he deal with the imagination in this situation?

As stated before, when he becomes aware of an impure though, he should immediately crowd out the thought with another vibrant thought that also engages his attention. In addition, he should take the advice of St. John Vianney to make a sign of the cross to drive away the temptation. And, as did St. Catherine of Siena when she was tempted by the devil with lustful images, he should say the name of Jesus repeatedly in the heart. An uninvited impure thought is not sinful, but once a person wills its continuation, sin enters in.

Another thing that can plague people in this area is the habit of impure fantasies, especially when they have a boring life. This seems to be a problem particularly when one is in bed waiting to fall asleep. Certainly developing the habit of meditative prayer during this time is a wonderful alternative to such fantasies.

However, there is also a way of sublimating these fantasies so that one can make the fantasy itself a prayer, or at least a motive for prayer. To do this, one simply meditates on the promise of an eternal marriage with God in the Kingdom. The Scriptures are full of such images. For example, in Isaiah 62:4, 5 we find:

No more shall men call you "Forsaken,"
or your land "Desolate,"
But you shall be called "My Delight,"
and your land "Espoused."
For the LORD delights in you,
and makes your land his spouse.
As a young man marries a virgin
your Builder shall marry you;
And as a bridegroom rejoices in his bride
so shall your God rejoice in you.[44]

Hosea 1 and 2 contain God's complaint against Israel: "The land commits great harlotry by forsaking the LORD" (Hos. 1:2). God leads her back to Himself and says after her return, "And I will betroth you to me for ever; I will betroth you to me in righteousness and

[44] New American Bible.

in justice, in steadfast love, and in mercy. I will betroth you to me in faithfulness; and you shall know the Lord" (Hos. 2:19, 20).

Ezekiel 16 is another example of God's spousal love for us: God passes by and sees Jerusalem, naked, by the side of the road. He takes her as His bride, dresses her, provides her with jewelry, and gives her a crown. Alas, she "plays the harlot" in her idolatry, and is richly punished. But in the end, God will forgive His unfaithful spouse and will restore His "covenant" with her "forever."

And, in the Song of Songs, God narrates His passionate love for His people, in a way that almost makes us blush. (For example, "You have ravished my heart, my sister, my bride, you have ravished my heart with a glance of your eyes, with one jewel of your necklace. How sweet is your love, my sister, my bride! How much better is your love than wine, and the fragrance of your oils than any spice! Your lips distill nectar, my bride; honey and milk are under your tongue; the scent of your garments is like the scent of Lebanon" [Song 4:9-11].) What a delightful thought—the union with God in a kind of marriage,

God who is more beautiful, more exciting, more charming, more faithful than any spouse we could ever imagine on earth.

What a glorious consolation to see an attractive person, and to be able to think, "Goodness, if that's how the copy looks, I can't wait to be married to the original!" Gender should not present a problem here, since of course, both men *and* women are created in the image of God. God, in His essence, is no more male than female.[45] Thus, a man picturing God as a beautiful woman is no less realistic than a woman picturing Him as a glorious man, although it challenges the imagination a bit more. The point is that good mental constructs that stir us to desire God more can be very worthwhile and help us turn away from sinful fantasies which lead us away from God.

St. Francis de Sales wrote that everything we see in this world should remind us of God. Why not a beautiful woman or man? Granted, we should not use the

45 "We ought therefore to recall that God transcends the human distinction between the sexes. He is neither man nor woman: he is God" (CCC 239). We call Him Father, as well we should, because He has a male role in relation to us.

form of someone we see often, lest we end up focusing on that person, rather than God, under their form. If we choose someone we have seen, and are not likely to see again, we will avoid this potential problem.

Now, to be sure, a fantasy focused on God can be taken to immoral extremes as well. If a person's thoughts become sexual so that he starts to become aroused, he should fast-forward through that to a more sedate sharing of affection. But, a chaste hug with the God who created in His own image the beauties we so desire on earth is a delightful thing. Ultimately, it is only union with this Beloved that will fulfill us completely as persons, and an imaginary hug with such a Lover is a powerful sign of that union and is more real than any earthly fantasy could ever be.

Worldly fantasies are about things that, at best, have happened or will happen for a time in this life. Godly fantasies are about what surely will happen, and continue without end, if we strive for the holiness to which God calls us. What will last forever is far more real than what is passing away.

We could say this sort of thing is just an extension of the prayer of St. Augustine:

> Late have I loved you, O Beauty so ancient and so new. … I rushed headlong after these things of beauty which you have made. … They kept me far from you, those fair things which, were they not in you, would not exist at all. … You have sent forth fragrance, and I have drawn in my breath, and I pant for you. I have tasted you, and I hunger and thirst for you. You have touched me and I have burned for your peace.[46]

Such a holy fantasy should make us want to move right into prayer, to strive toward that goal of marital union with God. It should inspire us to live a holy life, detached from the world,[47] attached only to the God of our dreams.

Looking

Many people tell me they struggle with looking at others in the street as sexual objects. In our oversexed

[46] St. Augustine of Hippo, *The Confessions of St. Augustine*, Book 10, Ch. 27. This quote is a slight variation from that found in the translation by John K. Ryan (New York: Image Books, 1960), pp. 254, 255.

[47] "Detached" in this context means "not dependent on worldly things."

culture, almost anyone can fall into that trap, so conditioned are we by the pansexualism of the media. The first thing to bring to mind in such situations is that this person is a child of God, someone with his or her own goals in life. This is someone worthy of love, not of use, to coin an expression of Pope John Paul II.[48]

Of course, the tendency to "use" is to look at all the different physical aspects of this person. However, if we learn to look at the eyes and then look away, we will elevate our looking to see a person, a complete person to which the eyes are the window.

Further, we can see this person as a wonderful sign of the glory of God. Rather than say, "I mustn't look lest I 'use' in my mind," better to say, "Here is another sign of God's beauty. I cannot wait to be united to Him." The *Catechism of the Catholic Church* teaches something similar:

[48] The Holy Father put forth the "personalist norm" as, "The person is a good toward which the only proper and adequate attitude is love." Stated negatively: "The person is the kind of good which does not admit of use, and cannot be treated as an object of use, and as such the means to an end" (Wojtyla, *Love and Responsibility*, p. 41).

> Purity of heart is the precondition of the vision of God. Even now it enables us to see according to God, to accept others as "neighbors"; it lets us perceive the human body—ours and our neighbor's—as a temple of the Holy Spirit, a manifestation of divine beauty. (2519)

Pope John Paul II wrote, "Beauty is essentially an object of contemplative cognition, and to experience aesthetic values is not to exploit: it gives joy."[49] In other words, admiring the beauty in another, without reducing that person to his mere sexual values, is a good thing, especially if it reminds us of God.

Are we exploiting such people when we "use" them to reflect on God's beauty? No more than we use a preacher when he speaks of God in an uplifting way. God Himself said to St. Margaret of Cortona, a beautiful, reformed sinner, "By your beauty I wish to encourage sinners to come to you, to be converted, and thus to give me greater glory."

[49] Ibid., p. 105.

What better way for one's gifts (beauty, charm, etc.) to be used, than to remind others of God?

By suppressing our tendency to look at an attractive person, rather than sublimating it, we may be doing something analogous to suppressing the sexual appetite, as discussed earlier. Doing so will not bring about the peace of chastity, but a tension in the psyche, ready to spring forth in an errant way in a moment of weakness.

To be sure, there are some people who are so provocatively dressed that it is hard to see them as a symbol of God. For such, it is best to look at their eyes and then look away and pray for their conversion. But many people we see in the street are just attractive, not sexy, and these we can see in the divine image.

Alas, we all breathe the air of the 21st century, in which exploitation is everywhere. Thus, whenever a person, especially a man, sees a member of the opposite sex (or, for a homosexual, of the same sex), he must have a way of dismissing such reflex thoughts by reason. When I see an attractive woman, I have developed the habit of saying to myself, "She's a person, a child of God," immediately to deflate any exploitive tendency from the start. Only then will I consider whether she can be seen as an image of God, or as one who needs prayers to rise above her immodesty.

There is another element which contributes to getting beyond visual exploitation, and that is to enter into conversation with the other person. Of course, this is not always possible, but there are certain situations where introductions and conversation are quite appropriate, even if optional. A number of people have told me that they have been able to sanitize their view of another by simply starting a conversation with the person. Certainly it is much easier to see someone as a person, rather than just a body, if one verbally communicates with her/him.

What, then, is "custody of the eyes"? It is keeping the eyes from checking out all the sexual values of one who is immodestly dressed when one has to work with such a person. An example would be a businessman discussing a project with a woman who is showing a great deal of skin. What he should do is make every effort to focus on the person as a whole, rather than on her sexual values. He does this by focusing on her eyes, the windows to the soul. He does this, not in a rigid, obsessive way, as if to say, "I mustn't look there or there," but in a way that is intent on seeing the whole person, including her sexual values, but truly trying to see the big picture.

If he sees her as a person, he can practice benevolence—Christian love—toward her, rather than exploit her visually. He tries to see her as God sees her. (If he can do so diplomatically and lovingly, he might even encourage her to protect herself from exploitation by covering up more.)

Pope John Paul II wrote in *Love and Responsibility*,

> The essence of chastity consists in quickness to affirm the value of the person in every situation, and in raising to the personal level all reactions to the value of "the body and sex." This requires a special interior, spiritual effort, for affirmation of the value of the person can only be the product of the spirit, but this effort is above all positive and creative "from within," not negative and destructive. It is not a matter of summarily "annihilating" the value "body and sex" in the conscious mind by

> pushing reactions to them down into the subconscious, but of sustained long-term integration; the value of "body and sex" must be grounded and implanted in the value of the person.[50]

In other words, he doesn't try to "artificially banish the values of 'body' or more generally the values of sex, to the subconscious, pretending that they do not exist, or at any rate have no effect."[51] He rather sees this person, one of God's creatures, as one he should love in a Christian way, who happens to have the values of body and sex.

[50] Ibid., p. 171.
[51] Ibid.

Chapter 6

Be Not Afraid

ONE OF THE things that bind people to their sexual sins is fear—fear of boredom, of loneliness, of not being able to break free. As our Blessed Lord and Pope John Paul II used to say, "Be not afraid!" Forge ahead. The difference between a saint and a sinner is that a saint is a sinner who never stopped trying.

Expect Psychological Withdrawal

Sometimes people are surprised by the sadness they feel when they give up not only sexual sins, but fine dining and drink as well. There should be no surprise. Just as an alcoholic or a drug addict experiences withdrawal when he gives up the subject of his addiction, so will a person addicted to sex experience withdrawal, and often a psychologically painful one at that.

When a person gives up alcohol or drugs, he is often warned that for several weeks, or even months, he will undergo a period of great desire for the substance and feel miserable. Knowing that, many are able to cope, with the realization that this misery will soon end. Likewise, the one who gives up immoral sexual activity, and perhaps fine dining and drinking as well, should anticipate at least six weeks of angst over his loss, but should take comfort in the fact that he will feel far better once he emerges from this dark tunnel. The recovered (or "recovering," as some prefer) sex addict is able to forget himself and love God and others freely. He is free from what St. Augustine called the "cruel slavery to lust."

When I gave up sugar, I was warned of this withdrawal and indeed experienced it. But, after six weeks, my health was so improved that I have never had the slightest desire to go back to it. Overcoming sexual addiction is not unlike this.

Evaluating Sins

One of the problems which often arise with those addicted to sex is that of evaluating their culpability for sins. The Church teaches that for something to be a mortal sin, three things are required: 1) serious matter, 2) sufficient reflection, and 3) full consent of the will.

As we saw earlier, the Congregation for the Doctrine of the Faith taught, "The moral order of sexuality involves such high values of human life that every direct violation of this order is objectively serious."[52] Thus, it should be clear from our previous discussion that fornication, masturbation, adultery, homosexual activity, and the use of pornography are serious matter.

With regard to masturbation a cautionary note is added:

> To form an equitable judgment about the subjects' moral responsibility and to guide pastoral action, one must take into account the affective immaturity, force of acquired habit, conditions of anxiety, or other psychological or social factors that can lessen, if not even reduce to a minimum, moral culpability. (CCC 2352)

Sometimes young people commit masturbation without knowing it is seriously sinful. In other cases, a

[52] *Declaration on Sexual Ethics,* henceforth, *DSE,* Congregation for the Doctrine of the Faith, 1975, no. 10.

person who has a habit of masturbation may well not give full consent when he masturbates.

What would be an example of a serious sin committed without sufficient reflection? If a person were to masturbate or use pornography without knowing it was wrong, or seriously wrong, this would be a lack of sufficient reflection. It would be a venial sin (although serious matter). If someone were to commit a serious sin by a reflex action, without even considering whether or not it was seriously sinful, this too would appear to be sinning without sufficient reflection, and thus a venial sin. If a person were half asleep or even partly sedated when committing the sin of masturbation, this would seem to involve a lack of sufficient reflection (and full consent) as well. Germain Grisez gives several other conditions for lack of sufficient reflection: "extreme fatigue, great pressure, distraction."[53]

What would be a case in which one sinned seriously without full consent? One might be a person doing something sinful with a gun to his head. Another

[53] Germain Grisez, *The Way of the Lord Jesus, Volume I: Christian Moral Principles* (Chicago: Franciscan Herald Press, 1983), p. 366.

might be the following: a person truly is working at his faith, meditating on Scripture or the life of Christ for fifteen minutes a day, attending daily Mass, confessing bi-weekly, doing spiritual reading. Let's say he had a habit of masturbation for the past fifteen years, and he has cut it down from once a day to once a week. He is praying for the Lord to take this sin away, but once a week, more or less, he feels a physical feeling come over him in various situations, and though he prays for deliverance right up to the last moment, he falls. Presuming true sincerity on his part, it would seem that this person does not give full consent.

Certainly, such a person should attempt to get up and go somewhere, even in the middle of the night, to break the mood. And it may be that he could benefit from counseling. It seems certain, however, that if he continues in his spiritual exercises, he will continue to reduce the frequency of this sin and eventually eliminate it.

Another case might be the man who wakes up in the middle of the night and has already, in his sleep, begun to masturbate. Once he is awake he should get up and do something, but if he prays for deliverance but continues what started in his sleep, it seems this would not involve full consent or sufficient reflection. Serious matter yes, but mortal sin, no.

The use of pornography generally involves much more of the will than masturbation. Intentionally going to a pornographic website would most likely qualify for full consent.

However, if a person is surfing the net and, let's say, by clicking the wrong thing finds he is at a pornographic website, this would not yet involve consent. He should, of course, click on some other web address right away. But, what if he lingers for, let's say, ten seconds before moving on? This would appear to be sinful, but not sufficient reflection or full consent. If he goes back to the site later, these two conditions would appear to be present.

I always encourage those who fall into masturbation, or any other sexual sin for that matter, to make one evaluation right after the event, as to whether he/she had sufficient reflection and gave full consent. Once they decide, they should not go back and re-evaluate it. The decision is made once, and the act should not be reconsidered later. If one did not have sufficient reflection or give full consent, it is not a mortal sin (even though still serious matter) and the person is free to go to Communion.

If there is true uncertainty as to whether a sin was mortal, the person should assume it was. He should say a perfect act of contrition (i.e., out of love), and plan to get to confession as soon as is reasonably possible. However, if a person is struggling to overcome an old habit of pornography use or masturbation, it is often rightly suggested that he go to confession every two weeks or so.

I don't think it is healthy to tell someone that any time he commits masturbation he should get to confession before receiving Communion "just in case." This negates the teaching on what is required for a mortal sin. If the person truly did not give full consent, it's not a mortal sin. He should simply live by that. Otherwise, he may begin to obsess over this sin and doubt he will ever win the battle. Progress in this area is often slow. It takes time to overcome a long-time habit of masturbation or pornography use.[54]

[54] For an excellent study of masturbation, see John Harvey's article, "The Pastoral Problem of Masturbation," at www.couragerc.net.

Don't Obsess

One case that may come up is that of the person described above, who is doing a number of things right, truly working at overcoming an old habit, and even making progress. But, because he has not completely overcome the sin of masturbation, he feels terrible. He begins to obsess about it and think he is lost. Someone like this needs to be reassured by a priest or mentor, not condemned. One who attends daily Mass, prays a good deal, and receives the Eucharist several times a week should be reminded of the words of the letter of St. Peter, "Love covers a multitude of sins" (1 Pet. 4:8).

He should be encouraged to keep trying and not become discouraged, since it is likely that these are not mortal sins, and he is on the verge of true holiness if he keeps up these spiritual practices and continues to grow in virtue. He should be reminded to think often about the benefits of chastity, as mentioned above, but not to think often about his sins.

As Bishop Sheen used to say, the devil is the great consoler before we sin: "It's not so bad.... God will forgive you...," but the great accuser afterwards: "You've sinned again. You'll never be free of this;

you'll never be saved." The Lord, on the other hand, is the great accuser before we sin: "Don't do this. You won't find happiness in this." But He is the great consoler afterwards: "Don't despair. I will take you back. Repent and find peace."

Sexual sins are generally sins of weakness, and they are not nearly so evil as sins of malice. Yes, they are serious matter, but even some of the saints struggled to put sins of lust behind them, including Augustine. (Augustine used to pray, before his conversion, "Lord, give me chastity, but not yet.") If a person is truly trying, he should be assured that God is pleased with his effort, even if he hasn't totally triumphed.

Fear of Loneliness

One situation that comes up fairly often is that of two people dating unchastely who have no intention of marrying, but one or both are afraid of being alone. They want to continue the relationship and are afraid to break it off lest they lose this person, who, they believe, is better than nothing. A person in this situation needs to get some support in doing what is right, namely, terminating the relationship. To do that, they must surround themselves with whatever friends they have, especially religious ones, and develop an active life.

They must realize that breaking away from this person is going to hurt, but it's like the alcoholic giving up drinking. At first it is painful, but in time it is very liberating. Clinging to a sexual relationship without a future keeps one from spending the time needed to seek a marriage partner and, of course, keeps one from God and His blessings. Like any addiction, it doesn't remove the pain of loneliness, it just postpones it. And, of course, it prolongs the separation from God which is like a slowly growing cancer of the soul.

Visits to the Blessed Sacrament can be of great help in this situation. Often when a person spends a half hour or more in adoration, he will come out feeling a bit more peaceful about a personal loss. It doesn't remove all pain, but it can soothe it, and in time it can make a huge difference.

Chapter 7

Extramarital Sins

Fornication and Foreplay

Fornication generally involves more of the will than masturbation. A couple who frequently fall into fornication should avoid situations in which this happens. Many say they want to avoid this sin, but they continue to return to the situation which has led to it before, namely, kissing on the couch. Returning to such a situation with the hope of somehow doing better this time is a serious sin against prudence and love of God, even if the couple does avoid fornication.

But it should be realized that not just fornication is serious matter. As we saw above, foreplay is as well.

Some have suggested that kissing should be postponed to marriage to avoid sexual sins. Perhaps most of the kissing being done nowadays should, but there is a presumption here that people are not capable of sharing tender, affectionate kisses. Affection is an excellent language of love and should be shared chastely in courtship. In fact, sharing chaste affection is an important element in preparing for a healthy marriage. When affection is seen as simply an introduction to sexual activity, there will be problems in marriage, because while a woman often needs affection, she does not always need or want sex.

For the committed Christian, and indeed anyone committed to chastity, kissing in courtship should be limited to saying goodnight and should be done standing. A man courting a young woman might kiss her tenderly, slowly, once … twice, and then hug her warmly. After this he says some complimentary words of love, says goodnight, and gives her a final gentle kiss.[55]

Again here, there is likely to be a period of psychological withdrawal if a couple moves away from fornication and/or foreplay to these scenarios, but it is a freeing thing. And it is an excellent way to prepare for a good, non-exploitive, Christian marriage.

[55] For a more in-depth explanation of all this, see my book *Christian Dating in a Godless World* (Sophia Institute Press, 2016), Chapter Two, upon which this paragraph is based.

Many couples have found this way of sharing affection in courtship a delight and an incentive to pursue real intimacy.

Women and Chastity

The sexual revolution was bad news for everyone, but especially for women. Why so? When a woman has sex with a man her body produces oxytocin, a bonding chemical (simply giving a feeling of well-being). She feels committed to him because she is more integrated than the man. A man's body produces oxytocin too, but his testosterone suppresses it. So, he does not feel so committed after he has sex. What often follows, then, is a relationship in which one person is committed, and the other is not. The woman tends to put up with his bad behavior because she does not want to go out and find someone else. The man, if he gives in to his lower nature, tends to be more and more casual about the way he treats her, because he discovers she'll accept it. The result is often bad treatment for women before marriage, and if there is a marriage, the same bad treatment or worse after marriage.

In the early 60s women began to agree more and more to men's sexual requests and thus began to be treated worse. By the early 70s many women had had enough and the feminist revolution began in earnest. The leaders did a marvelous job of identifying the problem, but their solution was worse than the problem. They decided that women could be just like men, asking men out if they wanted, paying for dates if they chose, and engaging in lots of sex, as long as they could have abortions to cover their mistakes.

Unfortunately, women can't enjoy casual sex without doing violence to their natures. This trend made the breach between the sexes even deeper. The divorce rate has doubled since 1960.[56] And, some estimates claim that as many as 50 percent of the members of the National Organization for Women are lesbians. Clearly, NOW's version of feminism isn't working.

Some contemporary writers have come to the same conclusion. Danielle Crittendon wrote in *What Our Mothers Didn't Tell Us: Why Happiness Eludes the Modern Woman*:

[56] Bridget Maher, *The Family Portrait* (Washington, DC: The Family Research Council, 2002), p. 94.

> The woman who comes of age today quickly discovers that she enjoys a ... guarantee of "sexual equality": the right to make love to a man and never see him again; the right to be insulted and demeaned if she refuses a man's advances; the right to catch a sexually transmitted disease, that might, as a bonus, leave her infertile; the right to an abortion when things go wrong, or, as it may be, the right to bear a child out of wedlock. Indeed, in all the promises made to us about our ability to achieve freedom and independence as women, the promise of sexual emancipation may have been the most illusory.[57]

In *A Return to Modesty,* Wendy Shalit points out, "The peculiar way our culture tries to prevent young women from seeking more than 'just sex,' the way it attempts to rid us of our romantic hopes or, variously, our embarrassment and our 'hangups,' is a misguided effort. It is, I will argue, no less than an attempt to cure

57 Danielle Crittenden, *What Our Mothers Didn't Tell Us* (New York: Simon and Schuster, 1999), p. 31.

womanhood itself, and in many cases it has actually put us in danger."[58] And, argue she does, quite effectively, using articles written by the liberationists themselves in *Cosmopolitan*, *Elle*, and *Mademoiselle*. Columnist Mona Charen opined some time back that the abstinence program *Best Friends,* which helps high school girls postpone sex, turn down drugs and alcohol, and develop real self-esteem, has given back to these girls their femininity.

Hephzibah Anderson, after years of having a good deal of sex, decided *not* to have sex for a year. She wrote this in her book, *Chastened*:

> As soon as I went to bed with a man, I'd lose any clear sense of perspective. I had constantly mistaken casual hookups for rose-tinted beginnings.
>
> However uninvolved I started out—however uninvolved it seemed I was supposed to be—I could not remain cool-headed (or cool-hearted) as the temperature shot up.

58 Wendy Shalit, *A Return to Modesty* (New York: Free Press, 1999), p. 12.

> To admit as much felt like letting down the sisterhood. I knew that as a woman my right to sexual expression was hard won, yet that ideal seems to have been watered down to become intimacy without intimacy. While it is billed as empowering to be able to love and leave a man like a man, to me it felt like I was denying a whole set of instinctive feminine responses, forcing myself to conform to decidedly masculine relationship ideals. And what a waste of energy all this weeping seemed![59]

The point is — women can regain their feminine dignity by living Christian chastity, and helping both themselves and their men to be saved. If men won't raise the culture to a Christian level (as indeed they should) then women can do it, as they have throughout the centuries. Bishop Fulton J. Sheen showed great insight when he said that the level of civilization of any society is always determined by the women. If women refuse to give in to premarital sex and insist

[59] Hephzibah Anderson, *Chastened* (New York: Viking, 2010), p. 30.

that men treat them well before and in marriage, they will raise the level of the whole culture.

Men and Chastity

Men have a good deal to gain from chastity, besides saving their souls (as if that weren't enough!), although for them the benefits are subtler. By committing to chastity and sticking to it, men build up their women more, and allow them to be confident, alluring, and mysterious. So often men who have the superior attitude which accompanies premarital sex are greatly disappointed to find their wives have become mousy little women. They seldom realize that they helped create this woman!

By honoring the virtue of their women, men help them to be real persons, with real minds and real wills, not the willful, angry woman who has rebelled against the bad treatment that so often accompanies unchaste courtships. The woman given over to the Lord is at peace with her identity, her husband, and the world. Additionally, a chaste man can live at peace with his appetites and avoid the selfishness which accompanies sexual license. He will be able to transmit the faith to his children in its entirety, because he has lived it. He will know the difficulties because he has faced them himself and overcome them. Blessed the children of such a father!

Premarital Sex and Divorce

The correlation between having premarital sex and subsequent divorce is known. According to a 1992 study published by the University of Chicago, men who have had premarital sex are 63 percent more likely to get divorced than if they had not. Women are 76 percent more likely to divorce if they have had premarital sex.[60]

Sometimes it is argued that the values of those who do not have premarital sex are likely to be more traditional and therefore more suited to permanence in marriage. True. We are not encouraging people to

[60] Edward O. Laumann et al., *The Social Organization of Sexuality: Sexual Practices in the United States* (Chicago: University of Chicago Press, 1994), p. 503. This is "regarded as the most authoritative and best designed recent survey on sex." As cited in Bridget Maher's *The Family Portrait* (Washington, DC: The Family Research Council, 2002), p. 63.

just avoid premarital sex while holding on to worldly values. What is being proposed is nothing short of conversion to Christ and His entire way of life.

Sexual intimacy during courtship, alas, is an excellent preparation for divorce.

Hooking Up

Ever since the sexual revolution which began in the early 60s there has been a growing movement toward blocking the procreative aspect from sexual intimacy. With the advent of "hooking up," mostly on college campuses, sex has been stripped of its other aspect, love. In this phenomenon we seem to have the arrival of a complete trivialization of sex, a cynicism about the possibility of graceful, intimate sex.

The *Catechism of the Catholic Church* teaches beautifully about sexual intimacy:

> Sexuality, by means of which man and woman give themselves to one another through the acts which are proper and exclusive to spouses, is not something simply biological, but concerns the innermost being of the human person as such. It is

> realized in a truly human way only if it is an integral part of the love by which a man and woman commit themselves totally to one another until death.[61]

One need not be a Christian to know that sexual intimacy has an inner truth that cries out for personal love and commitment. Its trivialization brings self-alienation along with the impersonal pleasure.

Do you want to live a life of genuine love, or would you settle for pleasure instead? St. John Paul II wrote, "Only the chaste man and the chaste woman are capable of real love."[62]

The Premarital Cohabitation Dilemma[63]

The number of couples who choose to live together without marriage has risen dramatically in the past fifty years from near zero to 60 percent. For

61 *Catechism of the Catholic Church*, no. 2361; quoted from St. John Paul II, *Familiaris consortio*, no. 11.

62 Wojtyla, *Love and Responsibility*, p. 171.

63 This appeared as an article in *Homiletic and Pastoral Review* in February 2021.

Catholics the percentage is almost 50 percent. One subject regarding this which has received little attention is that of the religious dilemma for a couple who claim Catholicism (or any Christian religion) as their faith.

Why Cohabit?

Why do couples choose to cohabit? Two out of three do so to test their compatibility with each other.[64] They assume that if they live together for a time they will be better prepared for marriage and will thereby avoid divorce. It is easy to see why that conclusion might be intuitively assumed.

Alas, it just isn't so. A large number of studies in the latter part of the twentieth century showed that living together before marriage *increased* the chances of divorce once married. However, a number of studies between 2010 and 2014 concluded that living together before marriage had no effect on

64 Brett and Kate McKay, "Should You Live Together before Marriage?" September 5, 2020, www.artofmanliness.com.

divorce rates.[65] Then, in 2018 Rosenfeld and Roesler carried out a new study that showed pre-marital cohabitation does indeed increase the chances of divorce after the first year.[66]

In an article about divorce rates for cohabitors which didn't consider Rosenfeld and Roesler, Brett and Kate McKay wrote,

> What's important to note here, however, is that while there may be emerging evidence that cohabitation isn't *harmful* to marriage stability, there isn't any evidence that it is helpful. It may not increase your chances of getting a divorce, but it doesn't at all *decrease* them, either.[67]

65 These studies included: Copen, Daniels, Vespa, and Mosher in 2012; Reinhold in 2010; Manning and Cohen in 2012. (From www.ifstudies.org/blog/premarital-cohabitation-is-still-associated-with-greater-odds-of-divorce.)

66 They agreed that chances of divorce were lower in the first year of marriage, but for every year thereafter the chances are higher. See article cited in footnote 65 above.

67 McKay and McKay, "Should You Live Together Before Marriage?" They added, "While more recent research showed that, even when controlling for selection factors,

Moral Issue

The first issue is that of pre-marital sex. As we saw earlier, Sacred Scripture has some things to say about fornication, that is, any sexual intercourse between unmarried persons:

> [Jesus said] from within, out of the heart of man, come evil thoughts, *fornication*, theft, murder, adultery, coveting, wickedness, deceit, licentiousness, envy. . . . All these evil things come from within, and they defile a man.[68] (emphasis added)

It should be clear from this that fornication is serious matter, the matter of mortal sin.[69] The Church makes this explicit:

---

married couples who had lived together before getting married" (or engaged) "had more negative interactions, lower interpersonal commitment, lower relationship quality, and lower relationship confidence," and were almost twice as likely to have at some point suggested divorce.

68 Mark 7:21-23; see also Matt. 15:19, 20.

69 For a sin to be mortal, three conditions must together be met: "Mortal sin is sin whose object is grave matter

> According to Christian tradition and the Church's teaching, and as right reason also recognizes, the moral order of sexuality involves such high values of human life that every direct violation of this order is objectively serious.[70]

St. Pope John Paul II taught this in different words in 1987:

> It is sometimes reported that a large number of Catholics today do not adhere to the teachings of the Church on a number of questions, notably sexual and conjugal morality, divorce and remarriage. Some are reported as not accepting the Church's clear position on abortion. It has also been noted that there is a tendency on the part of some Catholics to be selective in their adherence to the Church's moral teachings. It is sometimes claimed that dissent from

---

and which is also committed with full knowledge and deliberate consent" (CCC 1857).

70 Declaration on Certain Questions concerning Sexual Ethics (Congregation for the Doctrine of the Faith, 1975), no. 10.

> the *Magisterium* is totally compatible with being a "good Catholic" and poses no obstacle to the reception of the sacraments. This is a grave error. (Address in Los Angeles, September 16, 1987)

Being unable to receive the sacraments means one is not in the state of grace, but is in the state of mortal sin. This has serious implications regarding a person's candidacy for salvation.

Fatima visionary St. Jacinta Marto reported before she died that the Blessed Mother told her, "More souls go to hell because of sins of the flesh than for any other reason." She received that message in 1920. If one watches TV, reads the news, or uses the internet, it should be clear that sins of the flesh have multiplied manyfold since 1920.

Public Sin

It is not unreasonable to presume that a romantically involved couple who live together are fornicating. But there is more than the sin of fornication here. It's living in sin publicly. A cohabiting couple doesn't hide the fact that they are living in sin. That is far more serious than fornicating. They've gone public with it.

They are, whether they intend it or not, setting an example for others by their behavior. Although setting an example is usually far from their intention, it is *de facto* an example, one which they are willing to tolerate to achieve their goal.

In other words, the influence their actions have on their siblings, their nieces and nephews, their friends, etc. is something for which they are responsible.

How serious is that? Here is what Jesus had to say about it:

> Whoever causes one of these little ones who believe in me to sin, it would be better for him to have a great millstone hung around his neck and to be drowned in the depths of the sea. Woe to the world because of things that cause sin! Such things must come, but woe to the one through whom they come! (Matt. 18:6-7)

That's pretty strong, isn't it?

Now some may say, "Well, in this day and age, living together is hardly scandalous." It's true that due to the prevalence of this behavior, the number of those who might be scandalized is much lower than it was thirty or forty years ago. Nonetheless, it would be naive to think that no young person would be negatively influenced by a sibling or relative cohabiting. Our goal as followers of Christ is to set a different example than that of the world. Even if we prevented one child from pursuing cohabitation when he or she entered adulthood, it would be worth it to refrain from it ourselves.

THE DILEMMA

So here is the dilemma: a Catholic couple living together must either admit to themselves that they are publicly living in mortal sin, or they have to reject the biblical teaching that fornication is wrong. Option two would be unthinkable for a follower of Christ. Of course, a third option would be to try not to deal with the issue. But, in order to marry in the Church, they *have* to deal with it.

If they marry in the Church, and they marry another Christian, they participate in the sacrament of Matrimony. But to participate in a sacrament in the state of mortal sin is a sacrilege. So, it is important for the couple, or at least the Catholic party, to learn the Church's teaching on sexual morality and its biblical origins and to, as a minimum, embrace it as truth. If they do that, and confess their sins before the wedding, a sacrilege is avoided.

That doesn't solve the scandal issue, but it is a step in the right direction. What would be better is if the couple chose to live separately before the wedding to manifest their acceptance that pre-marital cohabitation is contrary to the biblically based teaching of the Church. A good number of couples have done that in the past. Some have said they are very happy they did it.

At the very least they should live in separate rooms and attempt to live chastely before the wedding. I have seen many couples do that as well. One such couple told their priest that doing so improved their relationship a good deal.

There have been a number of saints who cohabited for several years before their conversion. The most notable were St. Augustine (fourteen years) and St. Margaret of Cortona (nine years). After their conversions they prayed and did penance for many years for their former sinful life, which they deeply regretted. They should give us all hope.

If a couple *really* wants to avoid divorce, they should commit to praying together daily. A 1997 Gallup poll done by the National Association of Marriage Enhancement (nameonline.net) showed the divorce rate among couples who pray together regularly is 1 out of 1,152.[71] That's less than 0.1 percent. The national divorce rate is 40 percent (and perhaps more for cohabitors). There is no law against couples starting to pray together *before* they marry.

How much better to do something to prevent divorce that helps their relationship with God, rather than do what *harms* that relationship. The need for grace in marriage is far more important than testing compatibility so as to avoid greater odds of divorce. And, as we saw above, living together doesn't reduce those odds anyway.

Couples who are seeking to marry in the Catholic Church should use this time of matrimonial

[71] www/medium.com/@ajhillis/your-marriage-isn-t-christian-enough-78e32fa3cbd7.

preparation to take stock of their relationship with Christ and their level of commitment to live the Catholic Faith. The Lord promised us a cross if we would follow Him. Do we really want to follow Him?

Jesus expects a great deal. But He gives a great deal more.

Homosexual Activity

From what I have seen, breaking free from sexual sins is much harder for those suffering from same-sex attraction, since the desire is almost always psychological completion, not just physical or personal. Nonetheless, I have worked with scores of homosexuals who have overcome their involvement with illicit sex.[72] Some have done so only after years of struggle; others have had religious experiences which moved them rather quickly to sexual sobriety.

One of the common-sense steps for a person with same-sex attraction is to avoid homosexual bars and restaurants. Some say they just want a friendship from these places, but that is naive. Hardly anyone in these

72 For ten years, the author led a Courage group for those seeking to live chastely.

places is just looking for a friendship. Friendships with straight men are widely viewed as the best camaraderie for a homosexual. However, friendships with those sharing the same struggle and the same religious conviction can provide much-needed support.

This does not mean a formerly active homosexual can't associate with someone who is still in the lifestyle. He may be able to evangelize some of them. But his closest friends, the ones from whom he seeks support to strive for the Kingdom, should be those persons of faith who are living chastely, and especially those who are straight and living the faith.

Just about every person I know who has moved from homosexual activity to chastity has sought and found help through the groups mentioned earlier: Courage,[73] a Catholic ministry, or Sexaholics Anonymous,[74] or some other solidly Christian (or Jewish) group. Many have pursued individual spiritual direction as well.

73 www.couragerc.net.

74 www.sa.org for local meetings. For phone or online Zoom meetings, go to www.saphonemeeting.org/index.html.

Although it is not necessary to pursue reducing same-sex attraction, for those who choose to pursue it, help is available. Living Waters, a Christian ministry, has a program to help with this effort.[75] Also there is a counseling program working with this endeavor, Reintegrative Therapy.[76]

There is a self-help book for those who wish to reduce their same-sex attraction which has helped a number of people. It is titled *The Battle for Normality*.[77] There are also groups for parents and friends of those suffering from same-sex attraction. One for Catholics is EnCourage, a ministry of Courage.[78]

75 www.desertstream.org/welcome.

76 www.reintegrativetherapy.com/.

77 Gerard J. M. van den Aardweg, *The Battle for Normality: A Guide for (Self-) Therapy for Homosexuality* (San Francisco: Ignatius Press, 1997).

78 www.couragerc.net.

Chapter 8

A Warm, Chaste Courtship Is Possible

I HAVE WORKED with a number of unmarried couples who have struggled with chastity. After years of little success in helping them transition, I stumbled on an approach that has worked. I asked them to try an experiment for a month: to hug for five or ten seconds at a time, to step back, look at each other, and then hug again, and then again. They were to only kiss goodnight, tenderly, gently, standing up. In this way they experienced the closeness that every couple seeks.

I got one couple to try this mega-hugs, micro-kisses program for a month. After a few months they told me their sexual activity had stopped. They were being chaste.

Hugging is a great sign of solidarity, but it seems with all the emphasis on heavy kissing and sex, it's been forgotten. But hugging can be a more profound sign of intimacy than kissing. Alas, in many marriages there is little hugging because couples are so involved in more sensual activities during courtship that they totally forget about hugging.[79]

French Kissing?

French kissing (or tongue kissing) is a different genre than affectionate kissing. It's very sensual. It could hardly be called affection. From what I have seen, French kissing is the lynchpin of chastity. Kiss that way and all sorts of immoral sexual activity is likely to follow.

A couple may start out with affectionate kissing as a sign of intimacy. But when they transition from that to French kissing, the primary goal moves from intimacy to pleasure. As Aristotle taught, pleasure is good when it is associated with a (morally) good act; it is evil when associated with an evil act. Pursuing sexual pleasure outside marriage is seriously sinful, as we saw in Chapter Two (CCC 2351).

[79] I have written another book, *Christian Dating in a Godless World* (formerly titled *Christian Courtship in an Oversexed World*), which goes into more detail on chaste courtship. I will address chaste courtship here briefly, but more detail on this subject is to be found in the book.

Prolonged Kissing?

Affectionate kissing can be a way of manifesting a feeling of nearness, especially if it is brief. Pope St. John Paul II implied recognition of such kissing when he wrote, "Pressing another person to one's breast, embracing him, putting one's arms around him . . . certain forms of kissing. These are active displays of tenderness [or affection]."[80] On the other hand, prolonged kissing, even if done in a tender, affectionate way, is a way of enjoying each other, more than communicating nearness or solidarity. Furthermore, it is likely that the man (at least) will get aroused and seek to extend the arousal. Again, Pope St. John Paul II had apt words on this: "There can be no genuine [affection] without a perfected habit of continence, which has its origin in a will always ready to show loving kindness, and so overcome the temptation merely to enjoy."[81]

But even if he (or she) were not to pursue the continued arousal, prolonged kissing shifts the emphasis from giving to taking (even if not sexual), which is not

[80] *Love and Responsibility*, p. 202.

[81] Ibid., p. 207.

a good preparation for successful marriage. Taking, as opposed to receiving, is fundamentally selfish. Prolonged kissing is what might be called recreational kissing. It doesn't contribute to a deeper knowledge of the other, which should be the point in courtship. Even if it didn't result in seeking sexual pleasure (which is unlikely), it's not in line with the purpose of courtship.

Alternative to Prolonged Kissing

If a couple really wants to share affection without going beyond into pleasure-seeking, there is an alternative to prolonged kissing. One solidly Catholic man said he shared affection with his girlfriend by having her sit on the couch while he would lie next to her with his head on her lap. They would talk for hours as he played with her hand, kissed it, and talked the night away. He said they experienced real spiritual intimacy, so important to a future marriage. That's fine, as long as they don't change positions. That proved to be for him and his sweetheart far more personal and less selfish.

One married man told his friend, "Tell Fr. Morrow that Jan and I tried his head-on-the-lap idea last night. We loved it."

Chaste Courtship Successes and Failures[82]

A beautiful young woman from Long Island was blessed to have been raised in a solidly Catholic family and to have attended a truly Catholic high school. She made up her mind before entering college she wanted no part of premarital sex. After graduating from a Catholic college she took a job in Philadelphia. She prayed the Rosary daily and often attended Mass during the week in addition to Sundays.

At one point she met a man who seemed like a perfect match. He was polite, treated her well, and was Catholic. In fact, he attended daily Mass. She figured, "At last I found a man who will believe in chastity and with whom I will not have to fight all the time about that." After eight months of dating, he said it was time for them to have sex.

She told him, "This is such a disappointment. I thought you were a good Catholic and we were on the same page morally. I won't have sex with you."

[82] Adapted from the author's article, "Dating Is a Waste without Chastity," at www.Catholic.com (Catholic Answers).

"We'll either have sex or we will break up," he said.

She needed no time to think about it. "If that's the case, we'll break up." And so, they broke up. It hurt her a lot, because she really liked him. But she loved the Lord more. So, she wrote him off.

Eight months later he called and asked to see her. When they got together, he apologized for his worldly attitude and for being a hypocrite about his faith. "You were right, I was wrong. Our faith is empty if we don't pursue chastity. If I promise to embrace biblical values, would you consider dating me again?"

After giving it some thought, she agreed. They courted for a couple of years and then got married. Now they go to daily Mass and Communion together! They have four lovely children after six years of marriage.

One young woman who had rediscovered her Catholic faith met a guy in a pub. She found him to be a great improvement over her previous boyfriend. But he insisted on premarital sex early on. She consented and they became engaged after a while. Of course, she had to stop receiving Communion.

Perhaps she thought that once married she could return to Communion. But that didn't happen. Since her (Catholic) spouse had very little knowledge of or interest in the faith, he insisted on practicing contraception. So, she still wasn't able to get back to Communion. A good Catholic marrying someone who is not a practicing Catholic involves problems that are not solved once married. Not only is contraception a problem, but so are the number of children, sacraments, schools for the children, and Sunday worship as well.

The chastity issue does not come up only with insistent males. It comes up with females as well. One young man was quite interested in a woman, but she expected to have sex with him. He told her, "You're such a lovely woman. I was hoping we could date each other seriously, but if that's what you want, it just isn't going to happen." He broke up with her.

Another young man—call him Fred—a daily communicant, dated a woman for a while who seemed to be a solid Catholic. When she wanted to cut corners on foreplay, he was warned by his spiritual director that not only was that sinful, but also that more trouble lay ahead. His spiritual director was right. They got engaged, and a couple of months before the wedding she told him it was time to have sex. Being a daily communicant, he told her he had no intention of doing that. A big blowup followed, but he prevailed.

Unfortunately, he never told his spiritual director about that episode. Had he done so, his director told him later he would have urged him to run from this woman.

They married, and within a year she was urging him to pursue illicit sex. The marriage went spiraling downward from that point on and they divorced.

One young woman led a social life which was totally contrary to her Catholic faith. After some years of promiscuous living, she woke up one morning next to a guy whom she didn't recognize. She told her friends, "That's it. I'm not living this way anymore."

She went home, went to confession, and started to live her Catholic faith. She got some counseling from a Catholic counselor as well. She began to pray the Rosary and in time started to go to daily Mass.

After some time, she began dating a loosely Catholic man. Things went okay until after several weeks he tried to initiate sexual intimacy. She refused to go back to her former lifestyle, so she turned him down. A huge argument followed.

Two weeks later he admitted she was right. Her conversion would be a waste if she went back to her old way of living. They continued to date and after a couple of years they married. They pursued their Catholic faith together, and in time he started to attend daily Mass!

Both men and women sometimes tell me that it is impossible to find a potential spouse who will live biblical chastity. But that isn't true. I have officiated at a good number of weddings where the couples were not having sex leading up to the ceremony.

There was a time in the early Church when Christians had to renounce their faith or be put to death. Today for single Catholics, to live in the state of grace and have a solid friendship with the Lord, they are not being put to death for their faith, but they are asked to forsake their boyfriend/girlfriend for the Lord to date chastely if necessary. Compared to the early Church, the Lord is not asking much today.

Some say, "Well, Father, that is totally unrealistic today. It won't work." There is an apt quote from G. K. Chesterton that applies to this. "The Christian ideal has not been tried and found wanting. It has been found difficult and left untried."

If someone says, "Lord, I'm going to insist on finding a spouse who loves you and wants to live your moral norms," do you think God will say, "Hah! Good luck!"? I think He will rather say, "Great. I'll help you find someone."

So where are people going to find a potential spouse who is solidly Catholic and willing to pursue a chaste courtship? Catholic Match and Ave Maria Singles, to name a couple of venues. I have known a good number of Catholics who have found their spouses on these websites, and they are doing quite well. They wrote very specific profiles, indicating they wanted someone who was willing to have a chaste courtship and a contraceptive-free marriage. (One woman even asked any potential suitor to read my book *Christian Dating in a Godless World* and let her know if he would be on board with that before contacting her!) In other words, no nonsense. Although some slackers responded, the profile writers were able to weed them out fairly quickly.

Granted, a person needs to be cautious in pursuing online dating, and needs to take time in the courtship, but the potential for success is very good.

In his encyclical *Veritatis splendor*, St. John Paul II's encyclical on moral theology, he included a section on martyrdom (nn. 90-92). Why? Because if we are not willing to die rather than sin, we all have our price for betraying God.

As the above story of Fred whose girlfriend insisted on some compromises with chastity showed, if you compromise even a little in the courtship, more trouble will follow. It just doesn't work.

The women and men I know who have not compromised on sexual activity have all come out ahead. They didn't settle, and it paid off in a *very* good, lasting marriage. It makes sense, doesn't it? Those who pursue a chaste courtship are likely to develop the virtues of self-control, respect, patience, and non-exploitive affection. These are great ingredients for a successful marriage.

St. John Paul II wrote, "Chastity is a difficult, long-term matter; one must wait patiently for it to bear fruit, for the happiness of loving kindness which it must bring. But at the same time, chastity is the sure way to happiness."[83] Chastity may not be easy in our oversexed culture, but with the grace that comes through the Mass, the sacraments, and prayer, it *is* possible, and it is *very* rewarding.

83 Wojtyla, *Love and Responsibility*, p. 172.

CHAPTER 9

Marital Chastity

THERE IS A type of chastity for marriage as well as outside of marriage. It calls for the spouses to cultivate a profound friendship with each other and to avoid situations where their fidelity to each other could be compromised. This is in addition to several of the things already mentioned, such as refraining from the use of pornography, from masturbation, and from sexual fantasies. Another part of marital chastity is using natural family planning (NFP) rather than contraception.

The Difference between NFP and Contraception

A woman's body ordinarily produces one ovum or egg each cycle, and the normal cycle is about 28 days. An egg ordinarily has a life of 24 hours or less. The life of a sperm cell is usually five days or less. So, a woman is ordinarily fertile from five days before ovulation to six days after. By measuring bodily data, natural family planning can determine when ovulation occurs, and thus when a woman is fertile. This information can be used to either accomplish pregnancy or to avoid it.

Contraception, on the other hand, aims at preventing ovulation. A second function of contraception is to harden the uterine wall to prevent a fertilized egg from implanting there, should ovulation occur, and growing into a baby in the uterus. The latter is called the abortifacient function.

So what is the difference between NFP and contraception?

Sex Is a Unique Act[84]

The first consideration is the fact that the conjugal act is not some peripheral or merely biological act which does not engage the person. It is rather a highly personal act which touches a person at his very core. One can attempt to relegate it to the periphery of one's experience, but most people understand sexual intimacy as far more than a recreational activity. Of

[84] This appeared as an article by the author, "Contraception and NFP: The Difference," *The Priest Magazine*, June 1, 2016.

course, one may do violence to the essential meaning of a conjugal act by treating it as merely an act of pleasure without any other significance (as in "hooking up"). But most intelligent, reflective persons would see this as in fact "doing violence" to the very nature of sexual intimacy.

Our laws reflect this. To verbally abuse a child is considered bad enough, but to sexually abuse a child calls for prosecution and incarceration. And well it should. Our laws acknowledge that sexual contact is unique and has a profound effect on the person. Thus, arguments that contraception is analogous to using earplugs or using sunglasses fail to take into account that the sex act is unique insofar as it has a profound effect on the participants. It is a kind of core act, unlike hearing or seeing.

It is more analogous to a kiss, with all the rich meaning of that act. The kiss of Judas is considered deplorable because it made use of a sign of affection and love to turn Jesus over to His enemies. It was a shameful lie.

"Anti-Life" Mentality

Contraception is said to brand its participants with an "anti-life mentality," as Pope John Paul II wrote in *Familiaris consortio* (no. 30):

> Scientific and technological progress, which contemporary man is continually expanding in his dominion over nature, not only offers the hope of creating a new and better humanity, but also causes ever greater anxiety regarding the future. Some ask themselves if it is a good thing to be alive or if it would be better never to have been born; they doubt therefore if it is right to bring others into life when perhaps they will curse their existence in a cruel world with unforeseeable terrors. Others consider themselves to be the only ones for whom the advantages of technology are intended, and they exclude others by imposing on them contraceptives or even worse means. Still others imprisoned in a consumer mentality and whose sole concern is to bring about a continual growth of material goods, finish by ceasing to understand, and thus by refusing, the spiritual riches of a new human

> life. The ultimate reason for these mentalities is the absence in people's hearts of God, whose love alone is stronger than all the world's fears and can conquer them.
>
> Thus an anti-life mentality is born, as can be seen in many current issues: One thinks, for example, of a certain panic deriving from the studies of ecologists and futurologists on population growth, which sometimes exaggerate the danger of demographic increase to the quality of life.
>
> But the Church firmly believes that human life, even if weak and suffering, is always a splendid gift of God's goodness. Against the pessimism and selfishness which cast a shadow over the world, the Church stands for life: In each human life she sees the splendor of that "yes," that "amen," who is Christ himself. To the "no" which assails and afflicts the world, she replies with this living "yes," thus defending the human person and the world from all who plot against and harm life.

Of course, when a couple contracepts it is usually not because they are against life, or do not value life.

However, when they contracept, they slide into this negative view of human life, because the act of contraception is an effort to prevent a life from being conceived in a deeply personal human act.

It is analogous to what happens to a man who uses pornography. When a man looks at pornography, he ordinarily doesn't begin to do so because he holds women in low esteem or considers them as mere objects of enjoyment. However, once he has used pornography for a time, that is the mentality he emerges with. Subconsciously, he sees women as his playthings.

An Excluding Love

Vatican II's *Gaudium et spes* taught:

> [Conjugal] love is uniquely expressed and perfected through the act proper to marriage. Hence, the actions within marriage by which the couple are united intimately and chastely are noble and worthy. Expressed in a manner which is truly human, these actions signify and foster the mutual self-donation by which spouses enrich each other with a joyful and a ready mind. (GS, no. 49b)

This is an important phrase: "Conjugal love is uniquely expressed and perfected through the act proper to marriage." In other words, it symbolizes married love and forms the future of that love. So the symbolism of the marriage act has a formative power for the couple.

Now, the symbolism of contracepted sex is to communicate love toward one's spouse, but at the same time to exclude children. It is akin to what the French call an *egoisme à deux*. When a couple has sex, they not only symbolize their marital commitment of love, but they also form their love—in this case, an excluding sort of love.

It is not the intention to avoid more children that is the problem. That is an acceptable intention for just reasons. The problem is the act (of contracepted marital intimacy) itself in its rich symbolism which forms a love that excludes others.

It should be noted that natural family planning could be carried out with a contraceptive mentality, especially if the motive for using it is selfish.

Not Total Self-Giving

Pope John Paul II wrote:

When couples, by means of recourse to contraception, separate these two meanings that God the creator has inscribed in the being of man and woman and in the dynamism of their sexual communion, they act as "arbiters" of the divine plan and they "manipulate" and degrade human sexuality and with it themselves and their married partner by altering its value of "total" self-giving. Thus the innate language that expresses the total reciprocal self-giving of husband and wife is overlaid, through contraception, by an objectively contradictory language, namely, that of not giving oneself totally to the other. This leads not only to a positive refusal to be open to life, but also to a falsification of the inner truth of conjugal love, which is called upon to give itself in personal totality.

When, instead, by means of recourse to periods of infertility, the couple respect the inseparable connection between the unitive and procreative meanings of human sexuality, they are acting as "ministers" of God's plan, and they "benefit from" their sexuality according to the original dynamism of "total" self-giving,

> without manipulation or alteration. (*Familiaris consortio*, no. 32)

In other words, when using contraception the spouses are in essence saying, "I give you all of myself except my fertility," and "I want all of you except your fertility." This falls short of an authentically total self-gift.[85]

Other Differences

There are other differences between contraception and NFP, of a non-philosophical nature. For example, birth control pills (combination or mini-pill) are part-time abortifacients; depo-provera, another progestin

[85] See also from The Pontifical Council for the Family, "Vademecum for Confessors concerning Some Aspects of the Morality of Conjugal Life," February 12, 1997, no. 4. "The Church has always taught the intrinsic evil of contraception, that is, of every marital act intentionally rendered unfruitful. This teaching is to be held as definitive and irreformable. Contraception is gravely opposed to marital chastity; it is contrary to the good of the transmission of life (the procreative aspect of matrimony), and to the reciprocal self-giving of the spouses (the unitive aspect of matrimony); it harms true love and denies the sovereign role of God in the transmission of human life."

hormone injected every three months, is also a part-time abortifacient, as are the morning-after pill and the IUD; and, of course, in this age it should be mentioned that NFP is the only "green" (i.e., ecologically friendly) birth control method.

Meeting the Challenges of NFP Use

Occasionally a couple will tell me or another priest that they feel challenged to fulfill the requirements of abstinence when using natural family to postpone pregnancy, especially since nature increases libido during the time of fertility. Refraining from all sharing of affection during this time has not proven to be the best approach. A number of couples have found that pursuing that approach increases disproportionately the desire for closeness when a couple retires for the evening.

Some NFP users have discovered that sharing warm embraces or words of affection or complimentary expressions during the day can fulfill the need for intimacy quite effectively.[86] First among these would

86 For example, one husband regularly called his eighty-year-old wife "my bride." She loved it. Another husband often called his wife "my queen."

be 20-second hugs. Studies have shown that lengthy hugging (20 seconds or more) in marriage has a measurable beneficial effect on the partners, including the production of oxytocin (a bonding chemical), reduced blood pressure, and a reduction in cortisol (a stress hormone) in the woman.[87] Although they found that the effect in the woman is stronger, something happens in the man as well. One young husband told me, "I can just feel the tension of the workday melting away at about sixteen seconds into the hug." Couples should aim for at least one 20-second hug every day, but especially when they are practicing NFP to postpone pregnancy.

Marital intercourse is a wonderful way to express intimacy in marriage, but it's not the only way. Affection is also a wonderful love language and can lift the hearts of spouses in a deeply personal way. That bonding can make the marriage act that much more delightful when it takes place during the infertile times.[88]

87 According to a study at the University of North Carolina, this happens after 20-second hugs. See article at http://news.bbc.co.uk/2/hi/4131508.stm.

88 While practicing natural family planning to postpone pregnancy.

Conclusion

So, it seems that contraception has a powerful negative spiritual effect on those who use it, not to mention all the medical drawbacks it entails. Natural family planning, on the other hand, is a wonderfully "green" way of controlling family size, one that avoids all the negatives of contraception. It may involve a similar intention as in contraception, but an entirely different, profoundly formative act.

Is this an easily understood difference? No, it is subtle and requires some thought to grasp. But it is true, and understanding this is a key to marital happiness for those willing to embrace this truth and live it.

In an age when Man travels far and wide to find the beauty of an untouched lake, an undiscovered forest, a pristine beach, he is invited to find within, a natural beauty, an enriching harmony, a glory which he can honor, or a glory he can drag down into the commercial technology of his often self-alienating world. If he honors it, he can, for a time, become like God, symbolizing and forming a love which is total, superabundant, and creative. And, by so doing, he expresses his own inner glory and shares it with the world.

Chapter 10

A Failing Nation?

IN THE EARLY 20th century, J.D. Unwin, a British anthropologist at Oxford and Cambridge Universities, studied the centuries-long histories of eighty-six societies and civilizations. He published his findings in a 700-page book, *Sex and Culture*. He was curious to discover whether there might be a relationship between sexual license and the flourishing of a society. It seems that he was a rationalist, with no evident religious background. Briefly, this is what he found:

> The history of these societies consists of a series of monotonous repetitions; and it is difficult to decide which aspect of the story is the more significant: the lamentable lack of original thought which in each case the reformers displayed, or the amazing alacrity with which, after a period of intense compulsory continence (sexual restraint), the human organism seizes the earliest opportunity to satisfy its innate desires in a

> direct or perverted manner. Sometimes a man has been heard to declare that he wishes both to enjoy the advantages of high culture and to abolish compulsory continence. The inherent nature of the human organism, however, seems to be such that these desires are incompatible, even contradictory. ... Any human society is free to choose either to display great energy or to enjoy sexual freedom; the evidence is that it cannot do both for more than one generation.[89]

Canadian philosopher and blogger Kirk Durston drew the following from Unwin's book:

> If total sexual freedom was embraced by a culture, that culture collapsed within three generations to the lowest state of flourishing—which Unwin describes as "inert" and at a "dead level of conception" and is characterized by people who have little interest in much else other than their own wants and needs. At this

[89] J.D. Unwin, *Sex and Culture*.

> level, the culture is usually conquered or taken over by another culture with greater social energy.[90]

Pitirim Sorokin,[91] founder of the Harvard University sociology department, drew similar conclusions in his book, *The American Sex Revolution* (1956).

Kirk Durston brings up the research of contemporary literature carried out by Mary Eberstadt, which showed that greater sexual license brought down the family and resulted in "primal screams,"

> a massive increase in mental health issues, mass killings, and the rise of extreme identity groups at war with each other … all symptoms of a society rapidly spiraling into collapse. This appears to have greater explanatory power than Unwin's psychological

[90] Kirk Durston, "Why Sexual Morality May be Far More Important Than You Ever Thought," www.kirkdurston.com/blog/unwin.

[91] Sorokin died in 1968, shortly after the American sexual revolution had begun.

> suggestion, although the two may actually be closely related, given what Eberstadt shows.[92]

Durston concludes that God's laws regarding sexual morality may limit our short-term pleasure, but are ultimately about providing for our happiness. This, of course, is axiomatic in the field of moral theology.[93] The moral law is, in essence, the manufacturer's operating specifications. We are free to violate it, but if we do, we should not wonder if our lives are unhappy.

In the West, the sexual revolution began in earnest in 1960 with the advent of the contraceptive pill. If Unwin is correct in his conclusion that sexual license will bring down a civilization within three generations, we are already almost two generations toward that end. Turning this decline around is possible, but difficult. It calls for a small

92 Durston, "Why Sexual Morality May Be Far More Important Than You Ever Thought," commenting on Mary Eberstadt's *Primal Screams: How the Sexual Revolution Created Identity Politics* 2021.

93 The alternative is the error of voluntarism which holds that the moral law is based on God's will without reference to the flourishing of the human person.

segment of the society to be faithful to sexual morality and to pass it on to the next generation. These dedicated people have to be, in the words of Sorokin, "morally heroic" in the face of great persecution by the society at large.[94]

[94] See Ed Vitagliano "The Morally Heroic and the Rescue of Culture," December 2012, www.afajournal.org/past-issues/2012/december/the-morally-heroic-and-the-rescue-of-culture-heroic/.

CHAPTER 11

Summary and Conclusions

IN SUMMARY, THEN, a person suffering from sexual addiction should pursue the following steps:

- ✠ Work to convince his mind first, and then his appetite, his heart, that illicit sex will not make him happy.
- ✠ Seek God's help through prayer and a strong sacramental life and frequent Mass or worship. Read the lives of saints for inspiration.
- ✠ Find help in a mentor and/or support groups.
- ✠ Get therapy if necessary.
- ✠ Live a balanced life.
- ✠ Never let emotional love run wild. Work hard to bring it under the control of reason.
- ✠ Learn how to clean up his imagination.

- ✠ Substitute good fantasies for bad.
- ✠ When he/she sees an attractive person, see them as an image of God, his/her future Spouse.
- ✠ Fast weekly.
- ✠ Anticipate some withdrawal upon giving up unchastity, but realize that withdrawal only lasts a few weeks at most.
- ✠ Try not to obsess over sins, and evaluate a sin only once, rationally.
- ✠ Carefully avoid occasions of physical intimacy which lend themselves to unchastity.
- ✠ Realize that prolonging a sexual relationship for fear of loneliness keeps one from finding a marriage partner, and keeps one from God and His blessings, which far outweigh any temporary loneliness.
- ✠ For same-sex attraction, don't pretend that chastity and frequenting "gay bars," etc. can go together.

- ✠ If same-sex attraction is the problem, consider integrative therapy, and read good books on how to diminish homosexual attraction.

If a person is using pornography, he/she should, in addition to the above, get rid of all pornographic images and install pornography-blocking software on his/her computer. It would also help to study the Theology of the Body, either by taking a course on that subject, or reading literature on it, or both.[95]

Sexual addiction is a terrible cross, but the Church is here to help those who bear it. With God all things are possible.

> If the Spirit of him who raised Jesus from the dead dwells in you, he who raised Christ Jesus from the dead will give life to

[95] For Theology of the Body courses, see www.tobinstitute.org. For Christopher West's talks on Theology of the Body see www.youtube.com. For a free audio download go to www.corproject.com/your-body-tells-gods-story-mp3/. The simplest book on this subject is Christopher West, *Theology of the Body for Beginners*, (Wellspring, 2018).

> your mortal bodies also through his Spirit which dwells in you. So then, brethren, we are debtors, not to the flesh, to live according to the flesh—for if you live according to the flesh you will die, but if by the Spirit you put to death the deeds of the body, you will live. For all who are led by the Spirit of God are sons of God. (Rom. 8:11-14)

If one is married, he/she is called to marital chastity, which would include avoiding situations where one's fidelity could be at risk. And, marital chastity includes pursuing the "green" method of natural family planning to regulate the number of children in one's family.

The stakes for pursuing chastity are high for every individual. But, if Unwin and Sorokin are right, promoting a widespread return to a Judeo-Christian sexual ethic is essential to stop the decline of our Western civilization as well.

Prayer for Chastity

Father in Heaven, You have created us for love, and given our bodies nuptial meaning. You have enabled us to share in Your creative love in the sublime act proper to the sacrament of matrimony. Help us to see the beauty and dignity of this noble and profound act, and to never trivialize so precious a gift.

I firmly believe You are with me in this journey, that You will lead me home to sexual sobriety, if I am open to Your truth, Your grace, and Your ministers of love. Help me to be honest with myself, and with You, that I may know the peace of love rather than the chaos of unchastity.

Jesus, You showed us the truth about personhood in Your own life on earth. Help me to model my life on Yours, that within my own unique personality, I may come to imitate Your purity, Your love, and Your peace.

Spirit of love, help me to welcome You into my life, that I might live by Your gifts of wisdom, understanding, counsel, and courage. May they bring forth the fruits of self-control, modesty, and chastity in my life.

Mary, queen of peace and model of purity, bring my prayer to God, Father, Son, and Holy Spirit, that I might live always in His light, and rejoice forever in His love. Amen.

APPENDIX A

Two Stories of Overcoming Lust and Finding Peace and Chastity

1. Escape from Sexual Addiction

(These are true stories. Some of the incidental details have been altered to protect the privacy of the authors.)

Growing up, I was very timid and shy. I had a hard time making friends and keeping them. I preferred to be by myself, and I have always thought of myself as a loner. I saw others as very cruel, so it was easy to withdraw into my own world.

I discovered my sexuality, by accident, as a young teen. I guess I started masturbating when I was about 14 or 15 years old. It was exciting, and as I was not hurting anyone, I told myself, it was okay. Somehow, I knew better. I didn't know what the thing I was doing was called, but I knew I had to keep it a secret, because others would not understand. After each act, I would feel intense guilt, but the pleasure of the act made it something I was always dreaming about and desiring. I made sure to go to confession as often as I could, and the priests let me know clearly that this was not acceptable behavior in the sight of God or society.

I discovered pornography also by accident. At that time, there was no internet, no DVDs, no adult theaters that I knew of, or even imagined existed. I found some pictures from a porn magazine that had been left on a playground. The images were very exciting, and thinking back now, I know I was hooked on porn then. I wouldn't see any more porn until I left home and discovered how available it was. By that time, I was masturbating two or three times a day.

I didn't look to form relationships with anyone, I didn't need anyone. The only thing I would look forward to is the next issue of the porn magazine because by that time I was tired of the previous one. I had abandoned the Church for a time, but I knew I was missing something—the sacraments. I wanted to get away from this activity, but it had a hold of me so strongly, it felt like I would always be a prisoner. I started to go to weekly confession and Sunday Mass.

DVDs and the internet became available, and in my mind I would fantasize these women doing anything and everything for my pleasure without a worry that their needs or desires were met. They were, after all, very beautiful and were willing to expose themselves to me because of my value. Of course, after I was satisfied, reality would set in, and I would know in my heart that I had absolutely no value to anyone, and would sink deeper into myself.

The priests at confession always told me of God's love for me despite my failings, and continued to advise me to give up this activity and to pray to God and Our Lady for strength. I asked them if it was possible for me to get away from this for good, and I was amazed because I have never met a priest who didn't think that I could put this behind me through the grace of God. My prayer life had consisted of saying a few prayers in the morning and evening. I had grown up saying the Rosary with the family weekly, but had given that up when I left home. At the recommendation of a parish priest, I started saying the Rosary again and I tried to do it every day. It was difficult in the beginning, but I worked my way up to five decades a day.

The priest also had me read a card entitled "The Truth about Chastity"[96] several times a day. He also told me to read the lives of the saints and to try to get to daily Mass. I am still working on daily Mass. I go as often as I can, and I am praying for a way to get there every day.

The reading of the lives of the saints seemed to be the hardest thing to do. I saw the saints as winners—what would they have in common with a loser like me? Holiness was easy for them, I told myself. However, as I kept reading, I discovered that some of them struggled too.

I knew I had to do something. I had been stuck in this activity for most of my life. I could see myself dying still imprisoned in these sins. I started looking for books on the saints that were not dry. I looked for Catholic magazines to read and started reading the Bible, both Old Testament and New Testament, every day. I continued with the Rosary and getting to confession every week and Mass as often as I could.

[96] www.cfalive.com/products/truth-about-chastity.

When my priest first suggested that I read the card every day about four to six times, I was skeptical that this would do any good. I would read the card when I rose in the morning and when I hit the sack at night. Soon I could recite the contents of the card from memory, but it didn't seem to help much. I was trying to stop by myself as I always had done, and I might go for a while without sinning, but eventually, I would lose it and fall into sin hard.

My priest had explained that I couldn't muscle my way out of this, that the reading of the card would train the heart to know that I didn't need this sin. By reason I could convert my heart and give up the sin.

I worked on it and worked on it and would seem to be going to confession every week with the same sin to confess. I was, looking back on it, actually making progress, the frequency of the sin was lessening, and I was looking at pornography less and less, which was the key to overcoming this because the pornography was feeding the desire.

My priest was seeing progress, and told me so in the confessional, which was very helpful and encouraging. But I was still skeptical about achieving any real results.

I noticed I was making progress when I started reading the Diary of Sister Faustina along with my other readings, saying the Rosary every day, going to Mass as often as I could and weekly confession. After starting to read the Diary, I was absolutely amazed that there was even a possibility that God could or would love me enough to forget about my past life, even though I know that He died on the Cross for all of us.

I now try to say the Chaplet of Divine Mercy as often as I can. I am still working my way up to every day, and I am exploring some of the shows on EWTN as an alternative to the movies and TV shows I would normally watch.

The big break came a couple of years ago. It was a terrible year for me. Life up to then had been fairly easy. But that year I got in a car accident, my father had a heart attack and ended up in a nursing home, and my sister had a serious back injury. My uncle, who was suffering from dementia, got violent with the family and had to be placed in a nursing home; a tree fell on my car, doing serious damage; and it looked like I might lose my job. I think that God was shaking me and demanding that I WAKE UP.

I continued to read the card several times a day, and started to read a chapter of the Bible from the Old and New Testaments as well as a bit from the *Catechism of the Catholic Church* every day. I also got back to reading about the saints. The Diary of Sister Faustina really opened my eyes to how perfect God wants us to be. Even little sins offend Him greatly, but even that said, He wants to drench us in His Mercy.

As I write this, I haven't had a fall in five months, thanks be to God. While I do have occasional temptations, they are nowhere near as severe as they were when I was in the sin. I know that I will always have to be vigilant in this area, like a recovering alcoholic, but I never imagined that someday, through the grace of God, I would be free of this sin. I still shy away from people in a social setting, and am afraid that I will be exposed someday, but I am grateful to God and the many priests who were so kind and helpful through the years.

Now I fall very seldom into immoral behavior, perhaps once every four or five months. Thanks be to

God. With His grace perhaps some day I will stop falling into such sins completely.

I know I have to keep going forward. I have to be diligent and try to continue to grow in holiness—I have a long way to go. With God's help and the prayers of Our Lady and the saints, I hope to be counted among the obscure saints someday.

2. Freed from Lust

For a good part of my adult life, I have had a distorted view of the wonderful, God-given gift of sex. When I grew up there was no sex education in school and I didn't get it at home, so my distorted view was mostly formed by discussions with my teenage friends. This view carried on into my adult life.

In my early thirties, I had a deeply religious conversion and became a Christian. This changed my entire outlook on many things, including sex. But the problem was that I had many deeply rooted issues regarding sex that had become a part of me from my pre-Christian life. They didn't just go away automatically when I became a Christian.

As a Christian, my greatest struggle was with the sin of lust. Jesus said that "every one who looks at a woman lustfully has already committed adultery with her in his heart" (Matt. 5:28). I tried to resist and fight off my temptation, but I was most often unsuccessful.

When I converted to Catholicism and was able to participate in the Sacrament of Reconciliation, I confessed my sin of lust each time I went to confession, and was resolved not to lust again, but became quite disappointed with myself when soon after I gave in to it. It was a vicious cycle until one day I went to confession with a priest in a neighboring parish. I told him of my lustful sin and tendencies, and he gave me a card entitled "The Truth About Chastity." He instructed me to read the card daily. I did as he told me, and after a year or so, I began to see a change.

The same priest also encouraged me to frequent the Sacrament of Reconciliation more often and to attend daily Mass. I took him up on his recommendation.

Heretofore, when I went to confession, I confessed my bad behavior and was forgiven. This priest helped me to address the underlying desire that drove my behavior. By reciting daily the few lines on the card he gave me, I was able to develop the virtue of chastity. It didn't happen overnight, but I found that after over two years of faithfully reading and meditating on the card each day, I no longer wanted to entertain unchaste and impure thoughts. My desire had changed. The virtue of chastity had become more important to me than the fleeting pleasure of my lustful thoughts.

I am still tempted with impure and unchaste thoughts, but I vehemently resist them to keep them from becoming sin. My desire is to please my Heavenly Father and to become more like Jesus.

Appendix B

Courtship and Culture

SOME YEARS BACK I had the pleasure of helping a young woman who had lived with her boyfriend for three years, had a baby, and needed to rebuild her life.[97] Their relationship had deteriorated to the point where she had to find a new place to live. Her sister had taken her in temporarily until she could find a place.

She began to attend Mass regularly and go to confession fairly often, perhaps monthly. She prayed about fifteen minutes a day and she wanted to live in the state of grace. She had a few Catholic friends, but most of her friends were culturally where she had been three years before: not church-going, not pursuing virtue, not praying, and certainly not chaste.

But she was attracted to her newfound religion (she had been baptized Catholic but was never

[97] Adapted from the author's article, "Why 'Culture' Is the Key to Finding Your Future Catholic Spouse," *Angelus*, September 13, 2019,www.angelusnews.com/faith.

catechized). She wanted to live all of it, including chastity.

The problem was her culture. The vast majority of the people she knew were non-religious. Without the support of friends, without a Catholic or at least a strong Christian culture to support her new religious fervor, it was almost impossible to live out her faith.

The solution? She had to find new solidly Catholic/Christian friends. She could keep her old friends, so that she could perhaps bring them along on her new journey. But she had to find some new friends who would help her stay on track to complete her conversion.

When a friend told her that if she wanted to date, she should date a guy who would not insist on having sex with her, she replied, "There aren't any guys like that." If she continued in a worldly culture, she was right. But, there is a whole culture—admittedly small—of young men and women who are quite committed to living the faith, including chastity.

"So where do we find them?" ask some young Catholic women—and men too. Good question.

What a young woman (or man) should be seeking is not just a Catholic who attends Mass regularly, but one who has no intention to compromise his moral ideals no matter how much he likes a woman. So where does she meet a guy like that?

Oddly enough, it often doesn't begin with a guy but with a girl—or several. As we said above, she needs to have solidly Catholic friends to help her find a guy like that.

So where does she find this Catholic "culture"? I discussed this with our Catholic men's group recently, and we came up with a few ideas.

To find this new culture, she might get involved in a Bible study group, or a Love and Responsibility group (I know a man who met his wife at such a group in New York City), a pro-life group, or other such group which meets regularly. Friendships often come naturally for members of these groups. But, the focus should be on the topic first (for authenticity) and secondly on the big picture of being part of a religious culture.

Another place to meet chastity-minded young Catholics is in a class or workshop on the Theology of The Body, St. John Paul II's revolutionary treatment of love, chastity, and the nuptial meaning of the body. The Theology of the Body (TOB) Institute in Lima,

PA, has several week-long seminars in the vicinity of Philadelphia and Cleveland. There are also West Coast TOB events held from time to time, sponsored by Creative Catholic Works (www.creativecatholicworks.org). One woman told me she planned to insist on her future spouse listening to CDs on the Theology of the Body before they married.

These two are the only groups offering seminars on the Theology of The Body. The Cor Project holds TOB seminars across the US and in Canada, and they offer the possibility of an individual parish or group sponsoring some of their seminars. The group provides an event, Made for More, introducing the TOB and provides resources for attendees to continue their learning about TOB. In the past they have had events in Louisville, KY; Brighton, MI; Miami, FL; St. Louis, MO; Norman, OK; and Lexington, KY. There are other groups promoting this wonderful teaching of St. John Paul II. They can be found by entering "Theology of the Body Seminars" in a search engine.

I have been leading two single Catholic groups, one male and one female, in the Washington, DC, area for about 25 years. We pray together, have dinner, and then discuss the faith. (We meet in a restaurant.) The women's group was the first to form and they would invite "approved men" (good guys who were solidly Catholic but in whom the inviting woman was not romantically interested) to join them after an 11:30 a.m. Sunday Mass for brunch. This was one of several coed events they held each year, including the Epiphany Party, now in its 22nd year. (One year it drew 300 Catholics!) These groups are great places to find a Catholic culture.

Years ago one of the women in our St. Catherine Society was discussing the group with another member, saying, "Father insists on making chastity a part of this. I don't know if it will work." "Me neither," replied her friend. (Of course, without chastity it would be a Catholic Lite group.) Some months later they were nicely converted and pursuing chastity. Pursuing chastity is an integral part of our men's group as well.

There are any number of singles' groups in many metropolitan areas—especially in Washington, DC, and nearby. The more they are focused on learning the faith, the better. Catholic singles groups focused solely on meeting a member of the opposite sex are often not so good.

Now some may argue, "That's fine. But that culture may be small. How do I meet a good Catholic, a potential spouse?"

I know a good number of Catholics who have met their spouses on Catholic online dating sites. Catholic Match, Ave Maria Singles and Catholic Chemistry seem to be the best, but new Catholic sites may be appearing here and there. So, it might be best to just enter "Catholic online dating sites" in a web browser and see what comes up.

One lovely young woman put in her profile that she wanted any guy who sought to contact her to first read my book, *Christian Dating in a Godless World* (formerly *Christian Courtship in an Oversexed World*—same content). If he wanted to have the kind of courtship mentioned in that book he could contact her.

Well, at least one guy read it and told her he wanted to court that way. A little less than two years later, they married.

That is one way to cut through all the issues and make it clear you want a solid Catholic. There are other ways. For example, as another woman did, have them read my summary on a warm Christian courtship at www.cfalive.com/collections/leaflets/products/is-a-warm-chaste-courtship-possible. This is loaded with quotes from St. John Paul II's *Love and Responsibility*.

If you do go on a Catholic online dating site you might write a profile such as this:

> I take my Catholic faith very seriously and seek a man who does too. A chaste courtship is very important to me. If you attend Mass at least every Sunday, go to confession regularly, pray daily, and believe in the Church's teaching on marriage and accept *Humanae Vitae*, please contact me.

Now this article is written primarily from the point of view of a woman because there seem to be more women than men who want a hard-core Catholic mate, and because women have more to lose in the sexual revolution than men. Nonetheless, men could pursue a spouse online in an analogous way. The point is, if you do online dating, choose a Catholic site and don't be afraid to be specific. That way you avoid wasting a lot of time.

Online dating is not a panacea. You must proceed cautiously and take your time. But I have seen some wonderful results in the past.

Many young men and women do not realize that finding a solidly Catholic spouse is possible. It is. It takes a bit more effort than just settling for a faithless or weak-faithed person, but it is worth the effort. Marrying a strong Catholic can be a *great* help to your salvation. In the end, that's all that should count.

Final Notes

If you have success with any of the recommendations in this book, or any other approach in arriving at chastity, kindly consider sharing your story with the author that I might share it (anonymously, of course!) with others. My email is tgmorrow1@gmail.com.

Recommended Additional Reading

Delivered—True Stories of Men and Women Who Turned from Porn to Purity, by Matt Fradd (author), Joe McClain (author), Audrey Assad (author), & six more (Catholic Answers Press, 2014). Excellent inspiring stories of those who conquered *great* addictions to pornography and illicit sexual behavior.

About the Author

FATHER THOMAS G. MORROW is a priest for the Archdiocese of Washington (DC). He has a Doctorate in Sacred Theology (STD) in Moral Theology from the Pope John Paul II Institute for Studies on Marriage and Family. He has written several books: *Christian Dating in a Godless World* (Sophia Institute Press, 2016); *Overcoming Sinful Anger* (Sophia, 2015); *Overcoming Sinful Thoughts* (Sophia, 2021); *Be Holy* (Servant, 2009); *Who's Who in Heaven* (Emmaus Road, 2012); *Fatima in Brief* (Catholic Faith Alive, 2017); and *Amazing Saints* (Catholic Faith Alive, 2018). He has written booklets on the Rosary (*World's Most Powerful Mysteries*), the Stations of the Cross (*A Disciple's Way of the Cross*), and on heaven, hell, and purgatory (*God's Wakeup Call*). These publications are available at www.cfalive.com.

Sophia Institute

SOPHIA INSTITUTE IS a nonprofit institution that seeks to nurture the spiritual, moral, and cultural life of souls and to spread the gospel of Christ in conformity with the authentic teachings of the Roman Catholic Church.

Sophia Institute Press fulfills this mission by offering translations, reprints, and new publications that afford readers a rich source of the enduring wisdom of mankind.

Sophia Institute also operates the popular online resource CatholicExchange.com. *Catholic Exchange* provides world news from a Catholic perspective as well as daily devotionals and articles that will help readers to grow in holiness and live a life consistent with the teachings of the Church.

In 2013, Sophia Institute launched Sophia Institute for Teachers to renew and rebuild Catholic culture through service to Catholic education. With the goal of nurturing the spiritual, moral, and cultural life of souls, and an abiding respect for the role and work of teachers, we strive to provide materials and programs that are at once enlightening to the mind and ennobling to the heart; faithful and complete, as well as useful and practical.

Sophia Institute gratefully recognizes the Solidarity Association for preserving and encouraging the growth of our apostolate over the course of many years. Without their generous and timely support, this book would not be in your hands.

www.SophiaInstitute.com
www.CatholicExchange.com
www.SophiaTeachers.org

Sophia Institute Press is a registered trademark of Sophia Institute.
Sophia Institute is a tax-exempt institution as defined by the Internal Revenue Code, Section 501(c)(3). Tax ID 22-2548708.